The Readies

The Readies
by Bob Brown

Edited and with an Introduction by Craig Saper

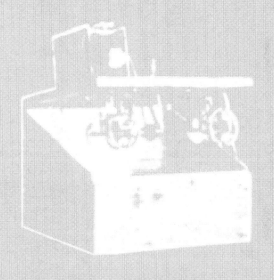

Roving Eye Press

Cataloging-in-Publication Data is available at the Library of Congress

22014940399

First published Bob Brown, Roving Eye Press, 1930
First published by Roving Eye Press, 2014
First paperback edition, 2015

Roving Eye Press
www.rovingeyepress.com
RovingEyePress@gmail.com

Introduction © Craig J. Saper, 2014

Book Design by Deborah Fay

ISBN: 0-692-21723-1 (clothbound)
ISBN-13: 978-0-692-21723-8 (clothbound)

ISBN: 0692388036 (paperback)
ISBN-13: 978-0692388037 (paperback)

ISBN: 0-692-21724-X (e-book)
ISBN-13: 978-0-692-21724-5 (e-book)

Printed and bound in the United States of America

Table of Contents

Bob Brown's Reading Machine: Abbreviated Writing and Browsers Fifty Years Before Txt, Tweets, and WWW.

The significance of Bob Brown's eerily prophetic *The Readies* now resides as much in media experiments as in literary studies. Taken as a whole, the manifesto speaks not only to students of modernism, but also, and perhaps more importantly, to a wider audience interested in media technologies' impact on a process we take for granted: reading.

This important manifesto, on a par with André Breton's Surrealist manifestos or Tristan Tzara's Dadaist declarations, includes plans for an electric reading machine and strategies for preparing the eye for mechanized reading. There are instructions for preparing texts as "readies" and detailed quantitative explanations about the invention and mechanisms involved in this peculiar machine.

In the generic spirit of avant-garde manifestos, Brown writes with enthusiastic hyperbole about the machine's breathtaking potential to change how we read and learn. In 1930, the beaming out of printed text over radio waves or in televised images had a science fiction quality—or, for the avant-garde, a fanciful art-stunt feel. Today, Brown's research on reading seems remarkably prescient in light of text-messaging (with its abbreviated language), electronic text readers, and even online books like the digital edition of this volume. Brown's practical plans for his reading machine, and his descriptions of its meaning and implications for reading in general, were at least fifty years ahead of their time.

These lines conjure a fantastic, if archaic, alternate world in their exhaustive descriptions of the reading machine's operations, the details seeming at once quaint, futuristic…and Kindle-esque: "Extracting the dainty reading roll from its pill box container the reader slips it smoothly into its slot in the machine, sets the speed regulator, turns on the electric current and the whole 100,000, 200,000, 300,000 or million words spill out before his eyes . . . in one continuous line of type . . . My machine is equipped with controls so the reading record can be turned back or shot ahead . . . magnifying glass . . . moved nearer or farther from the type, so the reader may browse in 6 point, 8, 10, 12, 16 or any size that suits him." (Use of the word "browse," incidentally, in reference to a graphical interface device rather than perusal in a bookshop or library does not appear again until the late 1980s, with the advent of database browsers.)

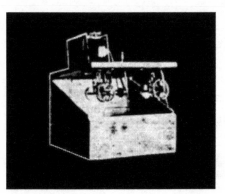

A prototype of the reading machine built by Ross Saunders, 1931c.

Brown's reading machine was designed to "unroll

Craig Saper

a televistic readie film" in the style of modernist experiments; the design also followed the changes in reading practices during the first quarter of the twentieth century. Gertrude Stein understood that Brown's machine, as well as his processed texts for it, suggested a shift toward a different way to comprehend texts. That is, the mechanism of this book, a type of book explicitly built to resemble reading mechanisms like ticker-tape machines rather than a codex, produced—at least for Stein—specific changes in reading practices.

In Brown's Readie, punctuation marks become visual analogies. For movement we see em-dashes (—) that also, by definition, indicate that the sentence was interrupted or cut short. These created a "cinemovietone" shorthand system. The old uses of punctuation, such as employment of periods to mark the end of a sentence, disappear. Reading machine-mediated text becomes more like watching a continuous series of flickering frames become a movie.

Recognizing punctuation marks as analogies for cinematographic zooms, close-ups, and special effects also allows the scenes in the Readies to function as an allegory for the process of reading in the age of machines. Readies sought to illuminate the form of a process rather than the form of a medium. Mechanical poetics (like Marcel Duchamp's descriptions of an impossible fourth dimension) magnify reading as a cultural technological medium without a single essential form. Using punctuation in this way—as a visual score rather than cues for reading aloud—and creating an endless array of portmanteau words, as Brown so enthusiastically does, makes literary interpretation problematic. Precisely because punctuation marks usually function to guide the voice to read prosody, the use of punctuation as analogies for motion and other optical effects moves reading from interpreting words in connection with an author's voice to emphasizing design, visual aesthetics, and movement. Readies do not efface expressivity, but they put the tone of *voice* in doubt. That kind of visual pun logic was common at the time in works by such artists as Duchamp and the Surrealists. Duchamp, a formative influence on Brown's experimental and visual poetry, designed, built, and found readymade machines that illuminated an alternative epistemology.

One could argue that the genesis of Brown's machine certainly includes Duchamp's machines and poetics. Artists like Raymond Roussell built their own Surrealist reading machines relatively soon after the Readies appeared. It seems fitting that Brown would call the processed texts the Readies, explicitly alluding to talkies and movies, and implicitly (and unintentionally) to *ready*mades. In light of his own claims in *The Readies* to do for reading what Pablo Picasso did for painting, or what James Joyce, Gertrude Stein, and e. e. cummings did for writing, one might call Bob Brown the Marcel Duchamp of reading.

The fascination with machine aesthetics was very

much of the moment in June 1930. In that issue of the modernist magazine *transition*, in which Brown announced his machine, the magazine's editor, Eugene Jolas, declared, "The mechanical surrounds us like a flood. The machine and its relations to man is doubtless one of the major problems of the age. Ever more accelerated becomes the tempo, ever more whirling are the pistons, ever more violent is the influence of this titanic instrument upon the thoughts and acts of man" (Jolas, 379).

In 1930, Bob Brown sent a manuscript of *The Readies* manifesto to Gertrude Stein. She loved his invention and laughed out loud at his playful presentation of plans and ideas. Stein soon wrote an essay celebrating "Absolutely Bob Brown, or Bobbed Brown," alluding to Brown's call to process all texts in a telegraphic cut-up style that eliminates all unnecessary words. In Stein's poetic allusion, readies' authors bobbed sentences like a flapper bobbed—cut short—her hair. Stein had cut her hair in a bob a few years before and saw the bob and Bobbed Brown as quintessentially modern.

Brown composed and published his manifesto— with an extended example of a readie, composed and bobbed especially for his machine—in the spa town Bad-Ems, Bavaria, Germany, during a rest cure. After his stay in Bad-Ems, he settled for about a year in Cagnes-sur-Mer, a Côte du Sur village near where Marcel Duchamp, Kay Boyle, and other artists and writers lived. Although some scholars now frame Brown as a dilettante of the European avant-garde, the modernists saw him as a precursor, and central innovator, to their revolution. Kay Boyle, who co-signed a "revolution of the word" manifesto in *transition* and twice won the O. Henry prize for best short stories, would describe Brown in a prominently placed 1959 *Village Voice* obituary as "one of the greatest innovators in writing (and printing)" whose *joie de vivre* inspired everyone who knew him. The expatriate modernists in Paris—especially those associated with *transition*—embraced *The Readies* project, with Number 12 in the magazine's "revolution of the word" manifesto ("THE PLAIN READER BE DAMNED") seeming to introduce Brown's efforts (Boyle, et. al., 12; all caps in original). In 1929, just before Brown's rest cure vacation in Bavaria, Harry and Caresse Crosby's Black Sun Press, in Paris, published his *1450-1950*, a book of hand-drawn visual poetry. One of those poems, "Eyes on the Half-Shell," was initially shown in 1912 (at least a year before Guillaume Apollinaire considered writing visual poems, or "calligrammes") to Marcel Duchamp, who published it in his *Blindman* in 1917. Brown would see in the "Calligrammes" (published in 1918) a realization of his desire for what literature could become, and he punned on "Apollinaris" mineral water, bottled eighty kilometres upriver from Bad Ems, by claiming to bathe in Apollinaire. Many decades later, Augusto de Campos, a co-founder of the International Concrete Poetry movement, republished Brown's *1450-1950* and introduced Brown's work as a precursor to concrete poetry (de Campos).

While an expatriate, Brown published approximately eight volumes of experimental poetry from 1929 until 1931—five in 1931 alone—including four volumes in which the visual design played crucial roles in the meaning of the texts. He continued to publish avant-garde works, advocated Surrealist writing, and published many volumes in popular genres throughout the 1930s. During those years, he simultaneously published tracts advocating communes and radical education, wrote Hollywood B-movie story treatments, and co-authored numerous cookbooks.

It was within the context of all this other work that Brown produced his manifesto. Even the dedication of the book to "all eye-writers" and "readers who want an eyeful" alludes to the recurring motif in his other work of the "celerity of the eye" (versus the "clumsy hand" turning pages), especially in visual poetry. In the manifesto's Chapter I, "An Eyeful," he illuminates that literary context all the way back to his reading Stephen Crane's "Black Riders" as a youth, and the socio-technological changes necessitating a more fitting way to read: "we have the talkies, but as yet no Readies." The chapter, written with a playful but passionate tone, demonstrates and explains the Readies' style, filled with what he calls "smashum" words, including a type of condensed anagram or portmanteau word, and a visual design in which "hermaphroditic hypodermic hyphen" replaces unnecessary words and chops up long words, all in parodies and experimental writing. Toward the end of the chapter, after singing the praises of Joyce and

Stein, he hints at the larger goal: "I know words can do anything, become anything, all I hold out for is more and better reading of the words we've got . . . reading will have to be done by machine; microscopic type on a movable tape running beneath a slot equipped with a magnifying glass and brought up to life size before the reader's birdlike eye, saving white space, making words more moving," using Brown's machine and his processed texts.

Chapter II's title, "A Two-Way Fish," alludes to a prop in a carnival game that allows the grifter to surreptitiously change a winner into a loser after the player-as-sucker picks a fish with a winning number (the shills win a few when the operator switches in the losing number for a winning number). The chapter begins with a series of notes before an extended two-columned experimental essay that seeks to challenge the for-or-against binaries usually found in critical essays and manifestos. The numbered entries in the two columns telescope autobiographical details into poetic allusions and dissect neologistic portmanteau words. The dramatization of the struggle to avoid critical judgment (or what we might now call logocentric meaning), with the two columns perhaps serving as visual and sound tracks, or two voices of dialog, ends with the phrase "apple sauce," at the bottom of one column, and "applause" at the bottom of the other. "Applause" is a visual pun, a condensed anagram or smashum of "apple sauce." The chapter reads like an absurdist play about modern reading.

Chapter III, "My Reading Machine," published in *transition* in the June 1930 issue as "The Readies," returns to an explanatory mode to suggest that the machine substitutes for the book as a distribution mechanism, and that the machine will shift reading away from cognition toward optics. He also returns to building a context for the machine in modernist culture, where "only the reading half of Literature lags behind, stays old-fashioned . . . cumbersome . . . bottled up . . . ." The chapter focuses on specific technical details and quantitative comparative analysis of reading and its mechanisms both in Brown's time and in his imagined future. The SteamPunk aesthetic, which imagines alternate histories of design as if contemporary technologies were invented in an earlier Victorian or Edwardian era, when steam was a dominant or prevalent energy source, would today embrace Brown's clunky futuristic machines, perhaps with the slightly modified name MachinePunk, reveling in cogs, gears, magnifiers, and spools running on a whirring electric motor. An alternate or counter-factual history of the reading machine's significance would describe the machine moving beyond a single primitive prototype with a small audience of modernist poets to have mass appeal and use. That alternate history of the machine highlights the aesthetic dimension and appeals to designers and artists outside of literary history.

Chapter IV, "Eye-Lingo," which goes on to describe his "inkless" revolution, seems prescient now, in the age of the Kindle, online texts, and ubiquitous handheld texting devices. Brown's reading machine will make "a need for new words" to work with the speed of the machine in portmanteau or "smashum" style, words like nowtime and machinewise, at the same time that conjunctions, articles, prefixes, quotation marks, grammatical marks, and other "bulky residue" will find little use. Although Brown insists that he is not inventing a new style of writing, but simply wants to prepare for the modernization of reading "at the speed of the day," the context of his own tastes and writings makes it easy for even the best critics, and sometimes Brown himself, to think of the project only in terms of the modernist revolution of the word and a "stab in the dark at writing modernly." Instead, the Readies function as a printed analogy for what reading will feel and look like "spinning past the eye out of a word-machine." He admits in this chapter that it is a "crude" attempt to simulate motion. (To resolve that shortcoming, this author has published online a simulation of Brown's machine, at www.readies. org, with the mechanisms built in an electronic simulation.)

The final chapter, "A Story to be Read on the Reading Machine," offers an extended example of a readie, which converts an otherwise unremarkable story into a cinematic imagist scene. Again, Brown's explicit goal is not to offer a new literary style but rather to suggest "the abbreviated dispatches sent by foreign newspaper correspondents to cut down cable expenses," as if one applied the technologies of the day to reading all texts, literary and practical.

One year after publishing his manifesto, Brown published an anthology of texts especially prepared for the machine. The later anthology included forty of his friends and fellow avant-gardists, with works by Stein, Boyle, and F. W. Marinetti. The anthology also included such Imagist poets as William Carlos Williams, with whom Brown had worked in the Grantwood Village art colony in 1916-17, and a sane Ezra Pound, who corresponded with Brown and the writers associated with *Others: A Magazine of New Verse* in those earlier years. The anthology's contributions, of uneven quality, have a giddy clubhouse feel and lack the coherent focus and serious intent of Brown's manifesto. Without any explicit editorial interference, and Brown only contributing an appendix (a condensed selection from *The Readies* manifesto), some texts seem more explicitly for the machine while others, like Marinetti's, seem to ignore or loosely interpret Brown's constraints. Some of the contributors, especially those *not* associated with modernist poetry, wallow in adolescent humor, as if baiting a fantasized censor with sexually explicit and racist language (One, in fact, was literally adolescent in perspective; written by Brown's teenage son, it describes his unpleasant first sexual encounter a year or two before, while they were living in Brazil.)

James T. Farrell, publishing one of his first stories in the anthology, later discussed how the Readies' constraints led to his staccato, short-sentence prose style in *Studs Lonigan*. Rather than employing a non-representational style, Farrell (and others, including Boyle) had found in Brown's constraints a foundation for a politically engaged writing of the street. Likewise, Brown had championed the work of Farrell and other politically engaged writers as part of the revolution of the word. Brown saw his machine as a democratizing tool, with the style of the Readies bringing literature to a wider audience by virtue of its resemblance to styles of popular writing generally regarded as beneath even low-brow genre pulp fiction: linear single-line ticker-tape news reports, secret codes, and telegraphic communications. Brown's appendix for the anthology includes the third chapter from the manifesto, along with other autobiographical materials, explicitly setting the context of the machine in relation to his work in publishing and printing magazines, reading the ticker-tape as a stock trader, writing for pulps, book dealing, and advertising.

Most scholarship until now has taken the Readies anthology as a homogenous group of texts linked only to modernism's *transition* fringe, and has framed Brown as a dilettante and hack writer. But neither the perceived homogeneity of the anthology's readies nor the portrayal of Brown as a late-coming advocate of modernist poetry finds support in the historical record. As mentioned previously, the simulation of the reading machine and online publication of the anthology at www. readies.org allows readers to experience the Readies as Brown intended one to read them. It also allows readers to make their own judgments about

Craig Saper

individual readies and the anthology project as a whole. This author's "user's manual" on the website covers, in a fashion similar to Brown's manifesto, both the specific technical issues and consideration of the implications of publishing an electronic edition of *The Readies for Bob Brown's Machine*.

As described by Brown in his *Readies*, the machine was the size of a typewriter, run by electricity, and unrolled "one moving line of type before the eye, not blurred by the presence of lines above and below." He planned to print the type "microscopically by the new photographic process on a transparent tough tissue roll" and this roll, "no bigger than a typewriter ribbon" would unroll "beneath a narrow strip of strong magnifying glass." It resembled a microfiche reader, for which Brown started to apply for a patent, and it was specifically to "rid" the reader "at last of the cumbersome book, the inconvenience of holding its bulk, turning its pages, keeping them clean."

Eventually, one would be able to "radio" readies as easily "as it is today to [produce] newsies on shipboard and words perhaps eventually will be recorded directly on the palpitating ether." In this sense, Brown's work is an ancestor of the shorthand languages emerging around new media technologies (i.e., instant messages, emoticons, etc). The material conditions of type were also something he knew well, for he owned presses including "a monotype" from which he "watched molten letters pour through it into an endless stream of words" (Brown,

Readies for BB's Machine, 160). Photographic composition and the use of new machines, like the "August-Hunter Camera Composing Machine" (180), would allow for "a multitude of words" to be "printed in a minimum of space and yet readable to the naked eye" (180). Is there a cultural poetics of the technical apparatus involved in reading? Brown's machine as cultural poetics sought to alter the future lineage of the mechanical process of reading.

The fascination with machines as alternatives to codex and other traditional forms of representation was not new to the avant-garde poets and artists of that era. In the early 1920s, the Dadaist Tristan Tzara wanted to know if he "could transcribe at top speed everything that fell, rolled, opened, flew, and continued" within his head (Tzara as quoted in Caws 17, n. 17). In Cagnes-sur-Mer, where they both lived, Brown would often talk with George Antheil about Antheil's blaring wind machine, used in his composition Mechanism (1923). Anththeil, self-proclaimed "Futurist-terrible," provoked audiences to riot during the machine concerts; he also composed the music for Fernand Léger's *Ballet Mécanique* (1924), a film that celebrated the mechanical comedy and stunts rather than the naturalized dance found in traditional ballet. The shift from considering *Readies* as another attempt at experimental writing to absolutely "Bobbed Brown" reading changed the equation from an aesthetic experiment to an epistemological alternative. That alternative did not seek to eliminate expressivity. Rather, it sought to expand the possibilities of the lyric to include new forms of media technologies and machines.

The different reading technologies and practices that informed Brown's shorthand included a wide array of systems usually not considered in terms of poetic materiality: reading and writing technologies ranging from wartime code machines to cookbooks or party guides, from Hollywood movies to a wide spectrum of magazines. These were not simply the commercial foil that professional writers like Brown reacted against in fleeing toward experimentation. Rather, Brown's work demonstrates a much more nuanced connection between the cultural milieu and a type of reading practice peculiar to the twentieth century. The machine highlighted the peculiar ways of reading abbreviated code systems: you have to change your pace and focus. We find this abbreviated language in stock market tickertape, shorthand, technical manuals, recipes, and specialized actuarial and accounting codes that came into widespread use in the first quarter of the twentieth century, during an era when "streamlined" equaled "modernity."

Unlike some of the expatriates who worked with him, and who were practically starving while they honed their craft, Brown had already made and spent or lost three fortunes as a popular writer and successful publisher. He moved to New York City in 1908, with an emerging reputation as a writer but nothing in his pocket, and lived in Greenwich Village, at one point sharing a room with Eugene

O'Neil. In the aughts of the twentieth-century, he sold at least a thousand stories and story-ideas to the pulps and other pulp writers, including to H. L. Mencken, who, as an editor of popular magazines like *Smart-Set*, relied heavily on Brown for content. Ezra Pound, in a letter recommending to James Joyce places to publish, mentioned the magazine's call for "top-notch" work and that some issues were filled with "one hell of a lot of muck"; in spite of the "muck," they both published there (Pound, 18). Menken continued to publish Brown later in the more serious *Mercury*. Brown's house in the Grantwood colony would serve as a rehearsal space for the Provincetown Players as well as a publishing center for the *Others* Imagist journal. At that point, in the teens, Brown had also parlayed his earnings as a writer into greater fortune as a stock trader. Finally, because of the pro-war hysteria and prohibition, Brown left the United States in 1918 and eventually settled in Sao Paulo, Brazil, where he built a very profitable publishing empire that would include business newsletters in four countries. In 1918, Duchamp and Mina Loy visited Brown in Latin America, and during the visit Duchamp cabled directions back to France for the creation of *Tu m'*, a pun-filled painting about mass production and the replacement of the painter with machines. Brown's publishing fortune would later fund his travels around the world, culminating in his arrival in France in 1928.

With the worsening economy in the early 1930s, and his unfortunate wrong bet on the stock market,

Brown would soon return to the States, broke, having to borrow the money for his family's voyage. His story does not end there by any means, but those subsequent chapters of his life are beyond the scope of this brief introduction to his most significant contribution to the modernist literary legacy: the readies and the reading machine.

As applications for his reading-machine platform, Brown's publications of *The Readies*, *Gems*, and *Words* represent one of the most significant contributions to the genre of literary works in which visual design and layout play a determining role in the meaning of the texts. His work was later seen by the Brazilian Noigandres concrete poets, the Beat poets, and L=A=N=G=U=A=G=E poets as an influence and precursor to their work.

Bob Brown became an avant-garde poet and impresario around 1912—well before the 1930 publication of his manifesto. From 1929 until his death in 1959, some considered him an important avant-garde writer and publisher. His connection to modernist writing, design, and publishing was neither fleeting nor limited to his few years as an expatriate in France. His more than fifty-year career as a writer had him serving as an exemplar for writers associated with both popular culture (movies, pulps, bestsellers, advertising copy, cookbooks, travel guides, magazine publishing, etc.) and avant-garde publishing. Brown's work also illuminates works in popular venues by writers like Joyce or Pound, who are usually studied in terms of experimental writing, and writers crucial to avant-garde publications, like Boyle or Farrell, who are usually associated with popular and politically engaged work. The reading machine has aspects of both parodic performance-art stunts, in the style of Tzara, Duchamp, and Antheil, and a practical tool or product ready to serve a mass market (a precursor to microfiche, Google books, e-readers, and text messaging). It is a truism of literary and art studies that the avant-garde opposes, by definition, mass-marketed products. Can a parodic art-stunt also function as a practical tool? In theoretical terms, can an attack on reading practices and the book's form serve an audience of book readers of canonical text? Does Brown's project present an intentionally paradoxical formation or does it represent an unresolved contradiction in his project and career? While *The Readies* did not initiate an avant-garde group or movement, like Dada or Surrealism, dedicated to mechanical forms of reading and processed texts, it now serves as a kind of dubious manifesto presaging and engendering the digital revolution in reading and publishing.

Although *The Readies* created a sensation among the avant-garde and expatriates, and was greeted with the kind of enthusiastic praise that other more immediately influential manifestoes garnered, the limited run of 150 copies, with no subsequent editions until now, assured that it would pass into obscurity. The two other strikes against Brown—his huge success in popular genres of writing and the great variability in the types of his writing—have

Craig Saper

made it challenging for literary scholars to find a place for him in either modernist avant-garde circles or in popular culture studies of pulps, movies, and cookbooks. Brown's work as both popular writer and avant-garde innovator makes those genre lines, generally used to divide publishers' lists of books as well as scholars' areas of study (i.e., modernism, popular culture, film and media, digital media, conceptual art, cookbooks, etc.), an irrelevancy. With its publication now, and with the electronic version accessible to a wide audience, *The Readies'* significance in literary and artistic history and technology's impact on reading both become more apparent. This manifesto presents a clear and concise statement about the avant-garde's interest in preparing for changes in the sensorium and especially their fascination with the eye's importance in reading relative to the perceived dominance of aurality and interpretation. It also presents the practical side of the avant-garde's desire to intervene in the machinations of everyday life. What if a machine illuminated the visuality of reading hiding in plain sight? Bob Brown's manifesto answers that question and demonstrates its potential.

Works Cited and Further Reading

Apollinaire, Guillaume. *Calligrammes: poèmes de la paix et de la guerre 1913-1916.* Preface by Michel Butor. Paris: Éditions Gallimard, 1995 (initially 1918), published posthumously.

Boyle, Kay, et al. "The Revolution of the Word." *transition: an international quarterly for creative experiment.* Ed. Eugene Jolas. No. 16-17, Spring-Summer (June 1929): 13. One-page proclamation signed by Kay Boyle, Whit Burnett, Hart Crane, Caresse Crosby, Harry Crosby, Martha Foley, Stuart Gilbert, A. L. Gillespie, Leigh Hoffman, Eugene Jolas, Elliot Paul, Douglas Rigby, Theo Rutra, Robert Sage, Harold J. Salemson, and Laurence Vail.

Boyle, Kay. "In Memoriam, Bob Brown." *The Village Voice* (August 26, 1959): 4. This issue of the *Voice* is commonly available on microfilm spools (Wooster, Ohio: Bell & Howell).

Brown, Robert Carlton. "Eyes on the Half Shell," *Blindman*, No. 2 (May 1917): 3. Also see Brown's "Resolution Made at Bronx Park" on the same page.

Brown, Bob (he no longer published under Robert Carlton Brown). "Experiment," one page of hand-written poetic commentary on the revolution of the word with visual poetry. *transition: an international quarterly for creative experiment.* Ed. Eugene Jolas. No. 18, Fall issue (November 1929): 208.

---. *1430-1930*. Paris: Black Sun Press, 1929; a
later facsimile edition published with new title
as Brown, Bob. *1450-1950*. New York: Jargon
Books, 1959.

---. *The Readies*. Bad Ems: Roving Eye Press, 1930.

---. "The Readies," in a section titled "Revolution of
the Word." *transition: an international quarterly
for creative experiment*. Ed. Eugene Jolas. No.
19-20, Spring-Summer (June 1930): 167-173. In
the Contributors section of that issue, on page
396: "Bob Brown has now settled in Paris after
a long stay in Brasil."

---. *Readies for Bob Brown's Machine*. Cagnes-sur-
Mer, France, 1931.

---. *Words*. Paris: Nancy Cunard's Hours Press,
1931.

---. *Gems: A Censored Anthology*. Cagnes-sur-Mer,
France: Roving Eye Press, 1931.

---. "Letters of Gertrude Stein." *Berkeley: a journal
of modern culture*, No. 8 (1951): 1-2, 8.

Crane, Stephen. *The Black Riders and other lines*.
Boston: Copeland & Day, 1895.

de Campos, Augusto [One of the founders of the
International Concrete Poetry Movement].
"Bob Brown: Optical Poems," the introduction
to the Brazilian edition of Brown's *1450-1950*.
First published in Suplemento Literário de "O
Estado de São Paulo"/ Literary Supplement of

the newspaper *O Estado de São Paulo*. 9 January
1965. Later included, with several poems of
Bob Brown's from the Jargon Books Edition,
in the book *A MARGEM DA MARGEM (AT
THE MARGIN OF THE MARGIN)*. São
Paulo, Brazil: Companhia das Letras, 1989:
126-141.

Duchamp, Marcel. *Tu m'* (1918). Oil on canvas,
with bottle brush, three safety pins, and one
bolt, 27 1/2 x 119 5/16 in. (69.8 x 303 cm).

Dworkin, Craig. "Seeing Words Machinewise:
Technology And Visual Prosody." *Sagetrieb:
Poetry and Poetics After Modernism*, Vol. 8, No.
1 (1999): 59-86.

Dworkin, Craig. *Reading the Illegible*. Evanston,
Illinois: Northwestern University Press, 2003.

Farrell, James T. *Studs Lonigan; a trilogy*. New York:
Vanguard Press, 1935.

Ford, Hugh. *Published in Paris: American and British
Writers, Printers, and Publishers in Paris, 1920–
1939*, Foreword by Janet Flanner. Yonkers, NY:
Pushcart Press, 1980.

Jolas, Eugene. "The Machine and 'Mystic
America.'" *transition: an international quarterly
for creative experiment*, Ed. Eugene Jolas. No.
19-20, Spring-summer (June 1930): 379-383. A
quarterly (irregular) from the Summer of 1928
to June 1930, this was the last issue before they
suspended publication.

Kostelanetz, Richard. *The New Poetries and Some Old*. Carbondale, Ill.: Southern Illinois Press, 1991.

McGann, Jerome J. *Black Riders: The Visible Language of Modernism*. Princeton, N.J.: Princeton University Press, 1993.

McGann, Jerome. From "Composition as Explanation (of Modern and Postmodern Poetries)," in *A Book of the Book: Some Works & Projections about the Book & Writing*. Edited by Jerome Rothenberg, Steven Clay. New York: Granary Press, 2000. 228-245.

North, Michael. "Words in Motion: The Movies, the Readies, and the 'Revolution of the Word.'" *Modernism/modernity*, Vol. 9, No. 2 (2002): 205-223.

North, Michael. *Camera Works: Photography and the Twentieth-Century Word*. New York: Oxford University Press, 2005.

Others: A Magazine of the New Verse. Ed. Alfred Kreymborg from July 1915 (1:1) – July 1919 (5:6) in editions of 250-300.

Pound, Ezra, James Joyce, and Forrest Read. *Pound/Joyce; the Letters of Ezra Pound to James Joyce: With Pound's Essays on Joyce*. A New Directions book. New York: New Directions, 1967.

Rasula, Jed, and Steve McCaffery. *Imagining Language: An Anthology*. Cambridge, MA: MIT Press, 2001.

Rothenberg, Jerome, and Pierre Joris. *Poems for the Millennium: The University of California Book of Modern & Postmodern Poetry*. Berkeley: University of California Press, 1995.

Rothenberg, Jerome. *Revolution of the Word; A New Gathering of American Avant Garde Poetry, 1914-1945*. New York: Seabury Press, 1974.

Saper, Craig. *The Reading Machine*. http://www.readies.org, an online simulation of the machine designed for *The Readies for Bob Brown's Machine*, with contributions by the original authors. Readies.org, 2009. May 22, 2009.

Saper, C. "BOEYEK TREYEN ING" (designed by E. Tonnard), in *Image Process Literature*. Edited by Chris Burnett and Elisabeth Tonnard. Rochester, NY: Ampersand, forthcoming 2010.

Stein, Gertrude. *Absolutely Bob Brown, or Bobbed Brown* (unpublished). Printed by Claude Fredericks at The Banyan Press in Pawlet, Vermont, 1955. Gertrude Stein and Alice B. Toklas Collection, Yale Collection of American Literature, Beinecke Rare Book and Manuscript Library.

Tzara, Tristan. *Faites vos jeux, Les Feuilles libres*, No. XXXI (March-April 1923): n.p., as quoted in Mary Ann Caws, *The Poetry of Dada and Surrealism: Aragon, Breton, Tzara, Eluard, and Desnos*. Princeton: Princeton UP, 1970.

Notes on the Text

To preserve the look and feel of the original, a few notes appear here instead of within The Readies.

1. Much of the word play involves well known modernist writers, e.g., Proustly (for Marcel Proust) or Gert (for Gertrude Stein) on page 1 or Whitmanized (for Walt Whitman) on page 2.

2. Brown claims to have gotten the idea for his visual poetry from the blank page from *Tristram Shandy* [note Brown's typo in the title] on page 2. The visual poem below that citation uses blank space as a poetic element.

3. Typos often they seem intentional either as part of a portmanteau word or, in at least one case ("adriot"[sic]), a meta-commentary on an editor's adroit proofreading (and the tendency of some readers to read significance into typos). On page 13, and elsewhere, Brown directly addresses editors and proofreaders, but it is unclear whether he intends that the proofing will be "well looked to" or whether one should keep the apparent typos as part of the meta-commentary.

4. Brown mentions that the spools of reading materials will be available like safety razors (page 31) in stores and even in telephone booths. Although cell phones have made phone booths obsolete, those phones' ability to download reading fits perfectly with the vision of a future where texts are tele-vistically delivered over the airwaves.

5. Brown lists many authors, to the point that the extended essay reads like a catalogue of authors in relation to printing and literary design. He includes representatives from three groups: modernist artists and writers and other innovative writers; the authors of canonical literary works; and printers and designers important to the history of the Book. He singles out Anthony Trollope (1815-1882), on page 32, for ridicule. Trollope, one of the most respected and admired Victorian novelists, was often disparaged for his long-winded prose and prolific output. Brown takes aim at Trollope to suggest that modernity's demands, and the efficiencies of reading machines, will make novels in the future much more condensed than Trollope's.

6. On page 37, Brown mentions Caxton in a list of authors and printers involved in inventing the traditional notion of the Book. Caxton, the first English printer, lived in the early and mid-fifteenth century and began printing in England in 1476, after a long career as a merchant, trading wool, luxury goods, and illuminated manuscripts. Typically stationers were early printers, and Caxton fit that mold, but he began his second career as translator and printer late in life. The first book printed in English, by Caxton, was the *History of Troy* (1473c.) and the second *Game and Play of the Chess* (1475).

7. In the same list of early printers and canonical authors, Brown mentions Jimmy-the-Ink on page 37. Brown referred to his friend and fellow pulp

writer in the first decade of the twentieth-century, William Wallace Cook, as a "modern day Jimmy-the-Ink." It seems likely that Brown uses the phrase to refer to a fifteenth-century type-founder and printer like James Grover, or a generic early English printer. But the placement of the pseudonym next to other founding printers and authors suggests a different allusion: Jimmy-the-Ink was also the pseudonym used by the author/illustrator James Daugherty, who was famous as a modernist painter and was a *New Yorker* magazine cover and cartoon illustrator. His illustrations in the 1920s often have elements of movement. While he was already considered a canonical illustrator and children's book author, an important figure in the definition of the modern Book, and later won both Caldecott and Newberry awards, he was not an early printer.

8. Bruce Rogers (1870-1957), mentioned on page 40, was one of the most important American typographers in the twentieth century. Known mostly for his use of typography in book design rather than typeface design, he designed more than four hundred books. Brown strategically places himself with the Gutenberg, Caxton, and Rogers lineage in the development of the Book, and beyond.

9. On page 32, "Chiswick Preß" includes the German character that usually replaces the letters ss. The Chiswick Press, publisher of William Morris and influential in English printing and typography, was part of the lineage of literary

meaning by typo-graphic design that Brown constructs in *The Readies*.

10. Racist and anti-Semitic words appear in Brown's example of a story to be read on his machine; see, for example, page 44. Perhaps this language is symptomatic of a failure and contradiction in the modernist project of the time, which sought to move beyond prejudice through the visual (see Michael North), perhaps it was an unfortunate anomaly and lacuna not central to Brown's work (see Craig Dworkin), or perhaps it was an intentional effort to produce a street-talk filled with expressivity and challenges to censors.

11. The note on pages 51 and 52 at the close of the extended essay is key to the project, as one can use the list as a guide to produce one's own readies (see, for example, Saper, 2010).

Author

Craig Saper, the author of Artificial Mythologies, Networked Art, and Intimate Bureaucracies, is currently a Professor of Language, Literacy & Culture at UMBC. He has edited multiple volumes including a forthcoming edition of Brown's *Words*. He is currently completing a biography of Bob Brown and an online simulation of Brown's reading machine..

THE READIES

BOB BROWN

THE READIES

BOB BROWN

ROVING EYE PRESS
BAD EMS
1 9 3 0

DEDICATED TO
ALL EYE=WRITERS
AND
ALL READERS
WHO WANT AN EYEFUL

CONTENTS

CHAPTER I

AN EYEFUL

The written word hasn't kept up with the age. The movies have outmanoeuvered it. We have the talkies, but as yet no Readies.

I'm for new methods of reading and writing and I believe the up-to-date reader deserves an eye-ful when he buys something to read. I think the optical end of the written word has been hidden over a bushel too long. I'm out for a bloody revolution of the word.

I don't mean maybe breakemup words I mean smashum (from the ancient Chinese ginseng root s a m s h u).

I Proustly rejoice in Jamesre.

I regurgitate with Gert.

I prefer E. E. Cummings word crumplets to R. L. Stevenson's crummy crawly Cummy scrawls. I say O. K. to Boyle. I like to read Hemingway, Carlos Williams, Sydney Hunt, Harry Crosby, K. T. Young, Links Gillespie, C. H. Ford, Herman Spector, Richard Johns, Norman MacLoed, Augustus Tiberius etc. I do not hiss in pronouncing Tzara's name. t r a n s i t i o n is my transit. I bathe in Apollinaire.

I'll be end man in any Rabelasian rhetorical rabble.

As a youth I peeped through a knot hole at Stephen Crane's „Black Riders", sniffed their jazzy inky blood as they read-raced by my bloodshot eye. I slaked word-thirstily in Blake. Grew rambunctious with Rimbaud. I Whitmanized.

From long gazing on the restful blank page for Poor Yorick in Tristam Shandy I began to get the idea. I learned to write m a r g i n a l i a without any text; I found myself flapping along quite happily without any words at all.

A dot and an angosturian dash with an hermaphroditic hypodermic hyphen is all that's needed nowadays, with maybe a word here and a blind spot there to help the heavy-heads out of their frowsy mental beds. Here's a poem, believe it or not:

```
                        ___
                     . — 00
(Explain yourself)
                      — (Title)
   . (Bullet)          — (Hyhen) 0 (Head)
                     00 (Heads)
                Bullet-Heads
                        ___
                     . — 00
```

Sure, break up the word and then throw all the broken bits away into a handy kaleidoscope. But keep a piece of each shattered statue, an arm of each Venus as a quarry specimen; preserve a hair of the dog you bit for publicity's shrinking sake;

dry a lee (now used only in the pl.), press it between the pages of a bibulous Bible, to serve as a shrivelled club-footed langwich for future arche-ologists to munch upon in the finale of the Last Days of American Pumpeana.

Demosthenes was a long time training before he knew enough not to swallow the pebbles. It took thirty years for Whistler to learn to throw a pot of paint at a canvas. It took Joyce about the same to touch off a word into a sky-writing rocket. He is said to have Shakespeared his time, maybe he's only skied it. It will take me all my little life to create a creation and my creation will be one word, many words, or simply more mea-ning and color of life, broadcasting with no words at all, and certainly reading done by machine in time with the age.

I operate on words. I gild 'em and then geld 'em (Ref. classical Quatre-arts Ball costume.) It's my specialty. I've been at it twenty-five years and never lost an Upper Case. For 8,890 nights I have lugged bulky, bulgy bundles of words home to dissect by violet ray before I went to bed. I get out my micro and my scope, breathe mystically 26 Abracadabras, one for each letter in the alphabet, and go to it with nothing up my rolled sleeves.

In my laboratory I have found that long-winded maundering words like Pseudepigraphous just go Puff when pricked with a pin, and pompous, prolix, sesquipedalian, Johnsonian inflations like infundibuliform when lightly poked in the bladder instantly inspissate and whortle down the funnel.

Nearly all clearly classical words fray easily, some wooly ones show undeniable traces of cotton and are a scant twenty=seven letters wide. Many make=believe altiloquential words merely shiver, shrivel up and subside when dropped into a specimen jar of alcohol, but most jolly ones ex= pand slightly and agitate the liquor like little ivory=toothed nigger boys diving for pennies. Weevil words bore. Wassail ones make whoopee. The assembled or modernly compiled word which stood the acid test best was the familiar five= legged one OKMNX.

But even for the sake of weariness I will not recount more of my recondite research. I only wanted that you should carry away from this chatty reading tonight the picture of a serious little word=wonderer at work among his retorts and cabalistic paraphernalia (Ref. to Rodin's The Tinker) dissecting words for you, TeeTer= ToTTering on Their T=bones, Playing PoPeep with sheePish PPPs, OOzing thrOugh adenOidal OOs, Zipping in Zig=Zags with the Zany Zeds.

Words and I are one. (Formula WW $+$ I $=$ 1)

I have only to bend my finger in a beckon and words, birds of words, hop on it, chirping.

There are midwives of the word and word specialists. To perform a Caesarian, a specialist is required. To deliver a norm head=or=foot=first all that's needed is a midwife.

Only savages and specialists bite off the um= bilical cord, midwives invariably hack at it with dull rusty knives at so much the yard=hour.

Hochachtungsvoll is a good Valkyrian German greeting, but it's long on letters, sort of teratological, like a medieval turtle lubbering along with its hard case carved full of mossy initials. Skoll (Scandinavian) or Ole (Spanish) is prefe= rable, or just Skolle: (Scanspan), quaint and friendly, Volapuckish.

The pidgin English rendering of Hamlet's „To be or not to be, that is the question", into „Can do, no can do. How fashion?" short=suits me.

I'll take RSVP at its face value. INRI, YMCA, SPQR, WCTU (deriv. W. C.) and other four- letter words I am willing to leave entirely alone, without any amplification whatsoever.

Shortening words I understand better than dragging them out. Eftsoons: linking letters in festoons I abhor. Underslung German dachshund, blown=up bumpy blimp, sausage words may be salivary to the starving mind but they're enough to shatter my meticulous monocle. Temptation to new word=bunglers is to make meaningless mouthings like „Our Exagmination Round His Factification for Incamination . . ."; the formula of officialdom used for years on French Railway conductor's tickets reads: „Decomposition de la Perception par Tarif", which is undoubtedly the key to much modern subconscious writing or unconscious humor.

From actual laboratory tests I have proved that long drawn=out gutta=percha words when stret= ched to the limit of elasticity invariably snap back and hit the experimenter on the nose with unexpected violence.

Cross-word puzzle fans blow the intellectual bellows of the time, fans with philological flares for flapping flaming fl-ashes back to ashes. They leave me cold; hearthless; cross. They've crossed my fingers for me. Crossed my eyes. Christ! how he must have suffered.

Making puns is as dangerous as making bombs. T.N.Tless, purely toothless, optical, gum-chewing puns as in opposition to the skull-grinning oral kind are not so risky, not so likely to go off in the hand. It is possible to turn out harmless eye-ticklers without undue hazard, though not without experience. Word-plays to fill the elegant eye more than to cram the merry mouth. Yet they may be judicially mixed while holding in a covered metallic receptacle at arm's length, as:

Gants	(Or, even)		gants
Pants	more Daring-		pants
Louis Quince	ly Experi-		louisquince
Your	(mental.)		your
Gants Louey!	Not	pants!	louey
Your	For		your
Pants Quince!	(Neophytes)	gants!	cants

Amateur alchymists while trying to magnetize mystical oracular utterances into glowing rosicru-tian word-formulas will find it convenient to hold their noses firmly pinched, owing to the noxious gases given off.

Fumblers for the Philosopher's Stone or stones and Elixir Vitae chasers will always take the Precatalanian caution of drawing the gants firmly over the pants and topsy-turvically.

Social experimenters in b e l l e s l e t t r e s will
realize that a taste for acquired words is as exac=
ting as a Bell Mare hostess who requires green
gloves to be worn throughout the olive course.
But don't let that make you a modest literary
wall=flower. Try all the new good forms; one at
a time or in the altogether; Romp with the
Rhomboids, take home a Hexagon to Give your
Hetaera the Gapes.

Bull=fights are optical grand opera; but just
because one Brooklyn boy has bit the sand of a
bloody arena in the s o l and s o m b r a of Sevilla
don't let that tempt you out of your eye=teeth.

Word=weaving makes pleasing patterns ref=
reshing to the patinaed retina, now that there's
not so much written oratory and reading aloud
of literary lullabies, except by radio at bed=time.

I fear for my word only when egotistical hoarse
bronchial word=busters forgetting their troches,
ride out brandybreathed, brandishing branding
irons at tropes, lassos writhing around their
hollow heads, screaming, „Write 'em, Cowboy,
write 'm."

Maiming words for some whets the appetite;
for me, wets my throaty=apple pie=eye. These des=
peranto language=melangers spik English writers
who threaten to internationalize the word horrify,
scarify me, as the Bolshevik Bogy of socializing
intent hobgoblined all virtuous kept women five
years ago. I tremble lest the Rooseveltian Haran=
gueoutanging Rough=riders of the Word bully us
back to the Hog=Latin of our youth for full esoteric

expression, or drop us into the inky pool of twinkling gypsy thieves jargon, or even invent for our punishment an international crook-word-code like the one uncovered in Brazil. The air about me becomes hazily thick with „finifs", „swell-mobs", „gaycats", and raucous uncouth racketeerings. I am stifflicated. Gagged by bushbeating wild word hunters, bound by a m b a g e s and bombastically flung into the see= thing alphabet soup.

I, who take my alphabet soup clear, daintily sipping it from the edge of the moon.

I, who had enough of Melanguages back in Mil= waukee when I was a bleating kid.

> Der cow hat over
> Der fence gejumped
> Und der cabbages
> Goddamaged.

What is that alongside the Halstead Street American lyrical purist speech of that pailer (ref. The unforgettable „Pail Period" in the U. S. A.) mauver, less decayed period (British: full stop) . . :

> Up through the alley
> And over the fence
> I got the can
> Who's got ten cents?

When I see words abused I volunteer, swear in instantly as an enforcement officer of the S. P. C. W. My word=sense shudders like a kicked sensitive plant at the sickening sight of over=

worded loads struggling up slippery verbiaged hills. I quiver when their brave bandy-worded little furry legs tremble. I'm afraid they'll slip back and suffocate in the green-whiskered Pond of Ezrasperanto Despond.

If it comes to words my heart is very tendrily. I cannot even bear to see them eaten. I weep long-bearded trickles from oystery eyes and turn from the slobbery sight as Lewis Carrol did and must do today over and over in his brillig grave.

As volunteer enforcement officer of the Society for the Prevention of Cruelty to Words I arrest all word-offenders and pretenders. I firmly ask the lowing carniverous judge to give them sixty days and seventy lashes with the dipthongs.

The Bible was once called the Word, and somehow I can't come to care how much the evolutionists monkey with that. But when it comes to regular human seven-day-a-week uninspired words I find myself of two minds and both of them lipstickily made up.

My answer to a Revolution of the Word is emphatically Yes to the No, No to the Yes, a determined Yezno — — — Oyez, Oyez, Oyez — — — Noyez.

The world is again threatened by an Uncivil War, already it is breaking up into small exclusive modern Browning Societies, word-diggers, mutual sentence — (back and elsewhere) — scratching cooteries. It isn't so much Browning who's to be feared, but the little Brownies who follow each other and yourself around.

2

Wasteful war! The words that will be spilt! And these mad revolutionists mean business, for several years they have been snooping around decapitalizing the whole vocabulary, lowering its case.

Oh, the words that will be spoilt: German sausage=word atrocities. I quiver=shiver. I rake= shake. Think of all those happy playful lisping harebell=lipped Mother=tonguetied words dragged down by leech=sucking Revolutionary Redun= dunces tugging at their tender=tipped dugs. I shudder at the thought=sight of it. Words orphaned, siamese=twined ones torn apart and thrown to grinning Siamese cats.

I won't have them exposed to the epidemic of onomatopeia, ravished by aneamic pernicious all- iteration germs. Snuffed out by Punditsters. Bitten by churlish word=lice. Punned over clodishly by Pierglass Ploughboys. I simply can't stand to see them honorificabilitainilatin=type=ized into hum= drum bores, I prefer them exactly as they are, happy, hedonistic thoughtless drumhums.

And yet somehow I want words to be made free. I only shudder at the thought of their being made free with.

The right of the writer to have his will with words is obvious. Words have always been de= fenceless and never wholly virginal. But I fear rotting, tumorish bad words may be slipped in (again, I don't mean curt, cute four=letter classics but fourteen=legged lecherridinous, centipedicular, ampapfibsimian enchondromatas) among my butter=cup=eyed innocents.

In a word — — Oh, my word.

I have ever felt cynical about the individual and collective helplessness of all m o t s. In my youth, ironing things out for myself I wrote **ironically** (following Carl Van Vechten's advice that the word irony should be carefully underlined):

Always my soft heart has beat with adulation
For people who edit and criticize writing
Worthy folk, going about wiping the noses of
    croupy phrases;
Tucking exclamation points into strange beds
Picking moth webs out of warm, fur-bearing
    sentences
And on top of that splitting cords of infinitives
To get up an appetite for a book review
I hold my breath when I come into the presence
    of these people
I feel highly humble

I'm still holding my breath and being humiliated; fearing what will happen when writers are let looser.

I'm afraid I'll lose my life-long companions, my play-mots of the dark glowering pause that is known as the laboratory hour; I fear something untoward will behap them:

I play with words
Tossing in the air an armful, as a child revelling
    in autumn leaves
Loving the crisp rustle as they cascade about
    my ears

Again picking them up as wet pebbles, aglisten
    on a cool sea beach
Making patterns of them — pictures — filling
    spaces with words as artists do with paints
I pet and fondle a sentimental word until it purrs
    and clash with a rough one till it growls
I am as human with words as I am with you
Never exploiting them
Never giving them an inch of advantage over me
I know words
And they seek me out
We are together
Important, both of us
And entirely useless
Unless you need the thing we give.

I repeat (having been set the example by our
recentest writers) that I love every lovable
Dublintender word James Joyce ever wrote and
I gurgle with delight in the joyous jugfuls of Ger=
trude Stein (As a Wife Has a Cow — a Love
Story, is a brimming pitcherful title). I know
words can do anything, become anything, all I
hold out for is more and better reading of the
words we've got. With more modern methods of
reading, words would take care of themselves,
the fittest would survive and bear fruity normal
new ones, with velvety fuzz covering the soft
spots in their heads and colicy didy smiles
lighting up their heavenly blue faces.

Writing must become more optical, more eye=
teasing, more eye=tasty, to give the word its due
and tune=in on the age. Books are antiquated
word containers. Quick=brown=fox=leaping=over=

Perhaps visual presence is what we've been looking through all along when it comes to words lazy=doggy, uptodate, modern word=conveyors are needed now, reading will have to be done by machine; microscopic type on a movable tape running beneath a slot equipped with a magnifying glass and brought up to life size before the reader's birdlike eye, saving white space, making words more moving, out=distancing the flatulent winded ones and bringing the moment brightly to us.

CHAPTER II

A TWOWAY FISH

Note: If there are sides to be taken on the question of Word Revolution I humbly ask to take both sides. Answering „Shall We Demand a Revolution of the Word?" I say Yezno! (from the Am. Fresno [a city], combined with Yes [a state of mind], and Zeno [Z as in Zebra and O as in naught.]) Oyez! Oyez! Oyez! NOYEZ! (from No as in Knowledge, with a left=handed but adriot allusion to the No in the French n o i s e t t e and the classical Japanese „No" plays.)

Note: If this by any of the odd chances of existence is printed in this modern era, the author humbly hopes that the proof-reading will be well looked to, as creeping mistakes cannot be detected with ease in such progressive writings as these, and said mistakes are certain to be taken seriously by some of the kind of Ouji=board readers one invokes in writing thusly. Typographical errors in modern publications have uselessly outworn many good and stoutly bound dictionaries.

Also, if a complicated corrected proof sheet to prove the author's Aegean labor is required to illustrate and further illuminate the following story, one can be instantly provided. (Vide: Unconstitutionality of ink-footed chicken-fight on Tribune press paper, of Horace Greely, the impeccable.)

To continue: Oyez! Oyez! Oyez! Knowyez!

I AM A TWO — WAY FISH

YEZNO	NOYEZ
For	**Against**
(Notes)	(Text)

A 2-way Fish is a Coney Island contraption used in a Prize Fish Pond; on one side it bears a winning number and on the other side a losing number, each concealed by a sliding tin tag painted fish color. The player of course is as unconscious of this as is the modern reader of other things.	A twiceweighed two-fister tooarmlong two-tooto and lovetoyou, two-toothy two trouty underoverishway Fish.

(1) **Thatcher:** It has been ascertained that our author lived at 290 Thatcher Avenue, River Forest, Illinois, from 1890 to 1907. Hence the rich reference to his rollicking carefree boyhood in the crucial formative period of his genius.

(2) **Larry:** Doubtless refers to the name of the grifter who operates the game and who reveals a winning number or a losing one at will, as we have learned. It seems miraculous yet Jonah couldn't do it, as our author playfully infers.

(3)**Verbunions:** Verb, into verbosity plus „I know my onions“, blooming into a fragrant word-flower suggesting the **vervain** — verbena.

(4) **bare fax:** Beatrice Fairfax the writer, rendered in delicious jazz motif.

(5) **Pax:** the disarmament note enters.

In Coney Catcher (1) Thatcher Cooney Canny Island glance eyebrowover the lowenbrau highbrow twoway twisty fisty 290 — 092 twofaced fish in the poley roley Pond. One side wins tother looses. Warrah. Godown Jonah Miracle Playboy.

Turn the crank (2) Larry.
This lazy-lady authoress zin a hurdygurdy hurry.
Zat's me. I nose my

(3) verbunions.
Cant makeup my catsup rouge-mind whats on it

(4) bare fax an' pock

an' pecks o' (5) Pax.

(6) **Flopside:** a variant of flotsam with pidgin English „topside".

No choose. (6) Flopside wins Jetsam loses. Loose change. All just blows down one windy nosey nostril an dup the tooting tother.

(7) **Not Fate. Fake.** Here Mr. Brown's righteous indignation gets the better of him and he delivers a well-deserved tirade on the ethical **mores** of Coney Island grifters.

(7) Not Fate. Fake. Ask Dad who runs the game.

(8) **Ask Dad. He knows:** **Hiram Watha:** The meaning of this delicious motif mingling the war cry of a well-known pipe tobacco with the majestic strophe of Longfellow's „Hiawatha" cannot be missed. „Hiram" also refers to the green-horn taken in by such obviously fraudulent practices. „Watha" clearly refers to the Waltham watch.

(8) He knows. Whatside topside bottomside scrapeside you inside outside upside downside furside Hiram Watha pipeside.

(9) **Shellshallow:** an echo of the Yankee shell game played with a

He wins both ways, ways that are deep and ways that are wary shocking (9) shellshallow shocked.

dried pea and three walnut shells. The author righteously denounces its hollow mockery.

(10) **Tender Button:** A gracious gesture calling attention to the title of a book by a contemporary modern.

(11) **Oddly-story:** Here a learned reference to the Odyssey i. e. Oddisy of Me.

(12) **Newt Neuter, frigged Newton:** Surely a portentious esoteric ref. of grave import to the initiated and recommende d for close study by all present-day Browning or Blueing Clubs. The stress seems to be laid on Newton's prior discovery of the Law of Gravity certainly not the childish Fig Newton of school days as some B. C. circles have advanced erroneously.

Like my winsome mind parted down the middle my middle yours truly (10) tender button Out of the insane salutarium solarium solaring above the solar plexipluvius I see word-

wise twoeye (11) oddly-story me see.

I'm Newt Neuter. I'm on both sides (12) frigged Newton applesas. I storyfence rubbernyneck stretched your nicked necking knuckly neck. Canook neck.

It's as plain as why what's that on your

(13) **Yis sid yir**: Occa⸗
sional precious passages
like this suggest spiri⸗
tual inspiration, almost
the divinely⸗driven wri⸗
ting of Blake. Here we
may assume that our
erudite author is **enrap⸗
port** with some choice
prankish spirits through
the ouija board, who
affect the adorable cant
of **nil fuit unquam sic
impar sibi** drug⸗store
cow⸗boys.

face. Yis I sid yir (13)
fice not chur fices.

§ **Melbolongetangy**: Ref.
Madame Melba's fa⸗
mous peaches. **Mel,**
Portuguese for honey,
deftly merged with
melange and suggest⸗
ing **lingerie. Bolonge**
from Bologna, an Italian
city. The word get plus
angry. Eva Tanguey.
The oolong tea tango.
Tanzy tea of Madame
Garfield's time. Balloon,
etc.

A slangwich § melbo-
long etangy
With a lugoobrious
lugged-in lugduni plot
that grows (1) gravy
toward the untoward
end.

(1) **Gravy:** See Dr. Blair's „The Grave", or any Presidential Thanksgiving Proclamation.

(2) **Tincked:** a cryptic nut to crack; this is believed to be a reference to tincture of iodine needed for the bruises made by Maudemule.

(3) Here the author bursts into high hyperbole.

(4) Obviously an overt allusion to prevalent French practice of guttersniping cigarette butts.

(5) References: Spoiled corned-beef fraudulently furnished by packers in Spanish American War. (See Upton Sinclair's The Jungle.) Also, last

Moredarn modearn Maudmulemad highbathatters of the Bank that Got Left — Leftover There, the mulekicked farsided behindbank Leftypitched lightningfork Tincked (2)

Juicy Joiced jousting Proustling jayhayyalejail (3) beerbeliedbird in the blueing handbush. A swell flathangnail on your flaphead.

But me no butts but botty bats in your bellyfree gutter. But you unbutton me. (4) Mummy!

Jock will beanwalk, Jock will beanstalk corned-licker talk wit hisern pisern ticklin Jock. (5)

— 20 —

phrase, Harry Lauder's inimitable Scotch Drinking Song.

(6) **Skookumlallies:** Am. Indian word for good raspberries, also suggesting the Mexican „tamales", best when taken hot.

(7) **Bloody:** An 'orrible hoath unedible in England.

(8) Allusion to the original Chevalier song „Knocked 'em in the Old Kent Road."

(9) Proverb from the Swedish.

(10) **Whora:** An ingenious combination of what Babylon was reputed to be, and the Greek proper name „Cora".

(11) **podgypetti:** contrived from Whora's pasty, pudgy body like spaghetti and the „Petit Pois" restaurant of lingering literary fame in N. Y.

(12) **tittette:** from titter and oysterettes.

Can do. No can do. How fashion? English pigeon? Hot Skookumlallies. (6)
Toedfashion toad I said hot pigeonbreasted pieface. Wanta hear about and about the burning

(7) bloody bushwackers.

I'll tell yer ear yer ear
(8) d'y'ear? Svenska

pika speilata naka. (9)

(10) Whora, great blon-

dette flapfat (11) podgypetty fogo'fat was in the current 1931 sixsex-

toetaptat (12) tittette, the Purple Floor and

(13) Here a high romantic note processionals in, reminiscent of „Beggars on Horseback", the „Little Church Around the Corner", and all to the appropriate strains of „Here Comes the Bride".

(14) **beanwalks:** (see above) the wordartist recalls the droll character of Jock and repeats the flute-like bean-note in this virile coloratura with the haunting charm of the Nibelungen Ring.

(15) Geo. Robey's famous Scrubwoman's Song.

(16) Dickens, that old curiosity-shop, inventor of the immortal Scrooge and Marley.

(17) **Fryher:** Now our learned language marvel, master of 34 tongues

Barn Door Gelett Burgess Saxaphonme 1391 tomorrow yet.

She tang a Tootsie Ittle Bideawee Bridetobe. Round corners (13) took telephoney poley catdog darknitey

fiteyflitey kikikitey (14) beanwalks evacucauliforner cation cauterized walling wellering welking walks. Oh my Yass

us Gals (15) must have Ourfuns. Oh, Knight o' Night Tales o'cats wit

to woo her mut to (16) Scrooge and Molly fieon-her and fryher

(17) that policanyPpup; their pornification

falls naturally into Platt=deutsch, a Low German tongue. How sonorously he slurrs the familiar **Freier,** Ger. for suitor or wooer.

(18) **Liberty Nation:** America, of course.

(19) the chess term „sta=lemate" happily married to the first mate of Moby Dick with a trusty belaying pin in his rusty hand.

(20) The heroine is ob=viously a petite Mexican hairless so he uses **Soya,** greatest of the Spanish beans, with a subtly flung **Soyanara** across continents to Japan, in pursuing his thematic sublimity.

(21) Ref: Brazilian poem by Gonçalves Dias, „**Minha terra tem pal=meiras Onde canta a sabia".**

(22) **Mexicanonocand=oodledo:** Here in one

round Carrie (18) Liberty Nation lampo=onification for justfuk=ation of Work in Progress. He mit her wit a (19) stalebone=whalebone=mate in is hie there.

(20) Soyabean out wit dedede mutt minha herrless tempalm arr=

aas (21) Mexicanonoc=

andoodledo to you. (22)

masterful Teocallian motifed word Mr. Brown sums up for us the action of the apologue thus far, the terminal eight letters reminding us vividly that the vigorous seat of action is still laid squarely like a Rhino's egg in the enchanting Land of the Chanticleer.

(23) **Godown:** a word used for warehouse throughout the Far East. A rhythm for a popular „Blues" melody lurks here.

(24) **Charicott:** a fruity word smacking of the vegetable kingdom — cherry plus chariot plus carrot all merged into the French haricot.

(25) **Springish sappy:** Bliss Carman's „Make Me Over", Mother Nature, when the sap begins to stir. Doubtless the author's undying tribute to the greatest of Canada Dry poets.

Godown sweet cheeses on got=your=gat=gut=gungadding kneezes an' du your biz your Lizzie biz on yur munny or your lifebouys

(DEEP BREATHING SEE SPACE)

Godown sweet (23)

(24) Charicott
Make me overnatured

(25) Springish sappy

(26) **Peppysdiarrhea:** Pepy's Diary plus Rhea, the offspring of Uranus.

(27) **Pupsnoze:** Reverent ref. to The Pope's Nose.

(28) **Boybowleggit:** the Bow=boy ingeniously and appropriately comb= ined with Liggett's drug= store.

§ We are utterly unable to trace the history of this regal tautological plum=pudding of words but it appears, to those of second sight who can read between the lines, to allude to the wellnigh insurmountable difficul= ty of eugenically mating an ordinary vulgar ad to a proper verb.

(69) **o':** here the cat=o' (Cato?) nine tales strain comes lilting back lum= inously through the Poet's Subconscious, and again a militant measure strides in.

(26) Peppysdiarrhea
Pups

(27) Pupsnozemizzling
Muskbasketer
Blind
Blueing in
One Boybowleggit (28)
Eye puggs puffed
Maskeenot the numer- ality, solely leather save me a shaveme, maleless hoarless,   frosty=biting

(§) one=legged=less twoless=legged
Polly put your leggin's on an' we'll all take a Promenlemonaid.

Harry=legged   hell   o' lonelymess o' (69) on= loveliness
One at a timpepiece Boyhoys Hands Off and Up! Hands Off Feet! Hans off the Hams! Change fingers! Harch! Harch in Finger

Ates! Reverse! Harch! Figure Hates! Mind-warts. (70) Motes in ze mind. Yours of the 6th Infant. received wit tinkletanks (71) drip-down downy leggish rungirl villainish purs-uitful white o' leg twinkles. Commet no Harry Kelly (72)

Panderangandamme (73) LukeMamGluke

It turneytables (74) out a umbiblicaul choirded

(75) chorus of mailmen

(70) **Mindwarts:** See: Watts, „On the Mind".

(71) The ghost of Milt Gross walks.

(72) Japanese word „Harikari".

(73) **Panderangandam:** Portuguese word for thunder.

LukeMamGluke: comp-ounded of the Am. vaudeville character Luke Mc Gluke and Madame Gluck, the opera singer.

(74) **Turneytables:** Knights of the Round Table after a Tourney, and the well-known rail-road mechanism for reversing engines.

(75) **Choirded:** cord, plus choir, plus dead. „March o' the Dead"? may we infer? (Author's note: Why not?)

3

(76) **Storked**: Symbol of a new birth.

(77) Adroit, masterful word-playing this! Munson Line boats run to the moonlit Southern Cross land of the Mons=oon.

(78) Kipling's classic „Under the Deodars".

(78) Kipling's classic „Under the Deodars".

(79) **Kloof:** South Afric=an Dutch word for hill; **scuppers** added — (Loo suggesting lee) hence lee=scuppers, and **Hatch,** a winking reference with the eye thrust half into the cheek, to the little known but truly rollicking sailor's chanty ending „that's my main Hatch. No more I'll go aroaming with you, Fair Maid, etc."

the pstman storked (76) inwit all wet.

A moonshiny moons=son toosoon struckit the Munsonliner (77) Toot sweet: Toot soon: and dey all downd=rownded wit der seadog buiscuits an' gutterper=ching overunderchews.

Der deerMable dragge=dunder (78) der udders

underdragged (78)

meowishly in ze (79) kloof-scuppers Hatch!

"§§⁰/₀&£ç&⁰/₀($$"§§??&§ ⁰/₀"$⁰/₀$&§Ç"Ç437£??§ ⁰/₀$$"&:Ç£?§⁰/₀—"&⁰/₀:& §)"?ÇÇ£?"$§⁰/₀$—

§§ Here the author falls into a slight but all too human error of judg=ment. Yes, his ears do deceive him. What he seems to hear is not the word „Applause", but the more expressively modern inexplicable ex=pletive:

APPLE SAUCE!!!

§§ Author's Note: What is that deafening sound I hear? Is it? Do my ears deceive me? Can it be:

APPLAUSE!!!

CAPTER III

MY READING MACHINE

The word „readies" suggests to me a moving type spectacle, reading at the speed = rate of the present day with the aid of a machine, a method of enjoying literature in a manner as up to date as the lively talkies. In selecting „The Readies" as a title for what I have to say about modern reading and writing I hope to catch the reader in a receptive progressive mood, I ask him to forget for the moment the existing medievalism of the BOOK [God bless it, it's staggering on its last leg and about to fall] as a conveyor of reading matter. I request the reader to fix his mental eye for a moment on the ever=present future and contemplate a reading machine which will revitalize his interest in the Optical Art of Writing.

In our aeroplane age radio is rushing in tele=
vision, tomorrow it will be a commonplace. All
the arts are having their faces lifted, painting,
[Picasso], sculpture [Brancussi], music [Antheil],
architecture [zoning law], drama [Strange Inter-
lude], dancing [just look around you tonight]
writing [Joyce, Stein, Cummings, Hemingway].
Only the reading half of Literature lags behind,
stays old=fashioned, frumpish,beskirted. Present
day reading methods are as cumbersome as they
were in the time of Caxton and Jimmy the Ink.
Though we have advanced from Gutenberg's
movable type through the linotype and monotype
to photo=composing we still consult the book in
its original archaic form as the only oracular
means we know for carrying the word mystically
to the eye. Writing has been bottled up in books
since the start. It is time to pull out the stopper.

To continue reading at today's speed I must
have a machine. A simple reading machine which
I can carry or move around, attach to any old
electric light plug and read hundred thousand
word novels in ten minutes if I want to, and I
want to. A machine as handy as a portable
phonograph, typewriter or radio, compact, minute,
operated by electricity, the printing done micros=
copically by the new photographic process on a
transparent tough tissue roll which carries the
entire content of a book and yet is no bigger
than a typewriter ribbon, a roll like a miniature
serpentine that can be put in a pill box. This
reading film unrolls beneath a narrow strip of
strong magnifying glass five or six inches long set
in a reading slit, the glass brings up the otherwise

unreadable type to comfortable reading size, and the reader is rid at last of the cumbersome book, the inconvenience of holding its bulk, turning its pages, keeping them clean, jiggling his weary eyes back and forth in the awkward pursuit of words from the upper left hand corner to the lower right, all over the vast confusing reading surface of a columned page.

Extracting the dainty reading roll from its pill box container the reader slips it smoothly into its slot in the machine, sets the speed regulator, turns on the electric current and the whole 100 000 200 000; 300 000 or million words spills out before his eyes and rolls on restfully or restlessly as he wills, in one continuous line of type, its meaning accelerated by the natural celerity of the eye and mind, [both of which today are quicker than the clumsy hand] one moving line of type before the eye, not blurred by the presence of lines above and below as they are confusingly placed on a columned page.

My machine is equipped with controls so the reading record can be turned back or shot ahead, a chapter reread or the happy ending anticipated. The magnifying glass is so set that it can be moved nearer to or farther from the type, so the reader may browse in 6 point, 8, 10, 12, 16 or any size that suits him. Many books remain unread today owing to the unsuitable size of type in which they are printed. Many readers cannot stand the strain of small type and other intellectual prowlers are offended by great primer. My reading machine allows the reader free choice in type-point, type seen through a movable magnifying glass is not the arbitrarily fixed, bound object we see impri= soned in books, but an adaptable carrier of flexible, flowing reading matter. Master compo= sitors have impressed upon apprentices for years that there is no rubber type. Well, now that the reading machine exists with a strong glass to expand or contract the size of letters, compositors can't ding on that anymore. Type today can be pulled out and pushed in as easily as an accordion.

My machine for reading eye=adjustable type is equipped with all modern improvements. By pres= sing a button the reading roll slows down so an interesting part can be read leisurely, over and over again, if need be, or by speeding up,a dozen books can be skimmed through in an afternoon without soiling the fingers, cutting a page or losing a dust wrapper. Taken at high gear ordinary literature may be optically absorbed at the rate of full length novels in half hours or at slow speed great pieces of writing may be reread and mused over in half life times if necessary. One so minded may continue to take his reading matter as slowly and dully as he does today in books. The underlying principle of reading remains un- affected, merely its scope is enlarged and its latent possibilities pointed.

To save the labor of changing rolls or records, a clip of a dozen assorted may be put in at one time and automatically fed to the machine as phonograph discs are changed at present. The Book of the Day or Book of the Hour Club could sell its output in clips of a dozen ready to slip into the reading machine. Maybe a bookclub offering a dozen new titles a day would result. Reading by machinery will be as simple and painless as shaving with a Schick razor and refills may be had at corner drug stores, cigar stores, or telephone booths from dawn to midnight.

With the present speeding up of publishing a machine is needed to handle the bulk and cut down the quantity of paper, ink, binding and manual labor now wasted in getting out twentieth century reading matter in fifteenth century book form.

The material advantages of my reading machine are obvious: paper saving by condensation and elimination of waste margin space, [which alone needlessly takes up a fifth or a sixth of the bulk of the present day book]; ink saving in proportion, a much smaller surface needs to be covered, the magnifying glass multiplies both paper and ink at no additional cost, the ratio is one part paper and ink to ten parts magnifier. Binding will become unnecessary, small paper pill boxes are produced at a fraction of the cost of large cloth covers; American publishers are discarding covers now to produce more and cheaper books, their next step will be to discard the Book itself in favor of the reading roll. Manual labor will be minimized. Reading will be less costly and may even become independent of advertising which today carries the cost of the cheap reading matter purveyed exclusively in the interests of the advertiser.

All that is needed to modernize reading is a little imagination and a high powered magnifying

glass. The Lord's Prayer has been printed in type
an inch high with illuminated initials as long as
your nose and bound in plush in elephant folio;
also, it has been etched on the head of a pin.
Personally I should have been better pleased if
Anthony Trollope had etched his three volume
classics on the head of a pin. Maybe no more trilo-
gies will be written when Readies are the vogue.
Anyway, if they are, they may be read at one
sitting.

By photographic composition, which is rapidly
taking the place of antiquated methods, type since
1925 has been turned out which is not readable
without the aid of a magnifying glass. The English
August-Hunter Camera Composing Machine fired
the first gun in this revolution five years ago.
Experiments with diamond type, like the old
Chiswick Preß Shakespeare Complete in one and
miniature books of the 64mo Clubs have already
shown what a multitude of words can be printed
in a minimum of space and yet be readable to the
naked eye. Even Cicero mentions having seen a
copy of the Iliad no bigger than his finger-nail.
Publishers of our day have perfected Oxford
Bibles and compressed all the short stories of De
Maupassant, Balzac and other voluminous writers
into single volumes by using thin paper. Dumb,
inarticulate efforts have been made for centuries
to squeeze more reading matter into less space,
(the Germans since the war publish miniature
Z e i t u n g s in eye-aching type to save paper and
ink costs) but the only hint I have found of
Moving Reading is in Stephen Crane's title „Black
Riders", which suggests the dash of inky words at

full gallop across the plains of pure white pages. Roger Babson recently listed the needed invention of a Talking Book in a group of a score of ways to make a million. But he missed the point. What's needed is a Bookless Book and certainly a silent one, because reading is for the eye and the INNER Ear. Literature is essentially Optical — — — not Vocal. Primarily,written words stand distinct from spoken ones as a colorful medium of Optical Art.

Reading is intrinsically for the eye, but not necessarily for the naked optic alone. Sight can be comfortable clothed in an enlarging lens and the light on a moving tape-line of words may be adjusted to personal taste in intensity and tint, so the eye may be soothed and civilized and eventually become ashamed of its former nakedness. Opticians have given many people additional reading comfort through lenses.

We are familiar with news and advertisements reeling off before our eyes in huge illuminated letters from the tops of corner buildings, and smaller propaganda machines tick off tales of commercial prowess before our eyes in shop windows. All that is needed is to bring these electric street signs down to the ground, move the show-window reading device into the library, living and bed-rooms by reducing the size of the letter photographically and refining it to the need of an intimate, handy portable, rapid reading conveyor.

In New York a retired Admiral by the name of Fiske has patents on a hand reading machine

which sells for a dollar; it is used in reading micro=
scopic type through a magnifier. Admiral Fiske
states: „I find that it is entirely feasible, by
suitable photographic or other process, to reduce
a two and one=half inch column of typewritten or
printed matter to a column one=quarter of an inch
wide, so that by arranging five of such columns
side by side and on both sides of a paper tape,
which need not have a width greater than one and
one-half inches, it becomes possible to present one
hundred thousand words, the length of an average
book, on a tape slightly longer than forty inches".

Recently the publishers of the New York tele=
phone book owing to the unweildy increase in the
ponderosity of its tomes, considered the idea of
using the Fiske machine and printing its product,
advertisements and all, in pages three inches tall,
in type unreadable by the naked eye. The idea is
excellent and eventually will force its way into
universal acceptance because the present bulk of
phone directories hardly can be expanded unless
hotel rooms and booths are enlarged. The inconvenience of searching through the massive volumes
of several boroughs has brought New York to the
necessity of giving birth to an invention.

But book me no books! In the Fiske Machine
we have still with us the preposterous page and
the fixity of columns. It is stationary, static, anti=
quated already before its acceptance, merely a
condensed unbound book.

The accumlating pressure of reading and writing
alone will budge type into motion, force it to flow
over the column, off the page, out of the book

where it has snoozed in apathetic contentment for half a thousand years. The only apparent change the amateur reader may bemoan is that he might not fall asleep as promptly before a spin=ning reading roll as over a droning book in his lap, but again necessity may come to the rescue with a radio attachment which will shut off the current and automatically stop the type=flow on receipt of the first sensitive vibration of a literary snore.

CHAPTER IV

EYE=LINGO

Revolutionize reading and a Revolution of the Word will be inklessly achieved. There have been rumblings of word battles from the eras of Rabel= ais and Shakespeare through the inarticulate arm= waving time of Whitman down to the deafening present. Creative writers have searched for new forms of word communication, methods of greet= ing more mental and aesthetic than dogs continue to employ so unimaginatively. Bawling creative Babes in the Word continue their struggle to shatter the filmy caul they were born with and get at the rosy nourishing nipples of their mother, the Sphinxlike Reader. Manifestos have been broad= cast in all tongues in all times, dating from the one God issued at the Tower of Babble, which carries on today in the Unknown Tongue by which Holy Rollers commune. Perhaps when we lift our creative writing heads too high again through the unexpected outlet of the Reading Machine God will come along and pie the type and we'll have to begin all over once more. But until then lets be busy at our Tower.

My reading machine, by its very existence, makes a need for new words and demands the deletion of some worn-out ones. The typewriter key-test of „Now is the time for all good men to come to the aid of their party" can be expressed with more interesting optical effect „Nowtime goodmen comeaid theirparty", or „Timegood mencome aidparty". No educated reading eye of this age cat_ches the little, useless, conventional conjunctions, articles, prefixes, suffixes, etc. unless they are needed for emphasis. The up=to=date eye scarcely sees the „thes", „ands", „ofs", „tos", „as", „ins", „thats", „fromits"; it picks out the meaty nouns, verbs and qualifying words so placed as to assume importance; only essential words get over to the practiced reading eye, the bulky residue is over-looked. Useless, unimportant sentence-encum-berers will be increasingly skipped and disregar= ded, until eventually they will not be missed at all by the eager eye in its excitement at witnessing a moving type spectacle, a READIE, performing before its Mind's Vision and the sensitive Inner Ear.

Already there is a tendency to do away with quotes in the French fashion and useless capital letters at the beginning of columns of poetry. The paragraph sign passed out long ago. All modern movements toward more effective simplicity are in the same sure direction; even the poet laureate of wordbound England at the end of his life has done his bit to loosen up the Language in „The testament of Beauty".

Let's see words machinewise, let useless ones drop out and fresh Spring pansy winking ones pop up.

Without any whirr or splutter writing is read= able at the speed of the day — 1930 — not 1450, without being broken by conventional columns confined to pages and pickled in books, a READIE runs on before the eye continuously — on forever in-a-single-line-I-see-1450-invention-movable-type-Gutenberg-Wynkyn-de-Worde-Jimmy-the-Ink- -- Caxton-though-Chinese-centuries-before-printed - thousand-page-books-on-silk-leaves-furnished-by- - local-silk-worms-no-two-leaves-tinted-alike - - - - printing-from-dainty-porcelain-type-same-stuff- - makes-teacups- - -dreams-Shakespeare-bending- - - over-workbench-making-language-laboriously- - - - bellowing-blacksmith-turning-out-grotesqueries-at-forge-all-onhisown-to-keep-UP-interest-in-job - - - Spenstream-of-lusty-steamy-bigfisted-word- - - - - moulders-flit-by- - - - - - -Rabelais-BenJonson-Dan Defoe-Sterne-WaltWhitman-GertStein-JimJoyce- - Stephen-Crane's-Black-Riders-Crash-by-hell-bent- - for-leather-uppercase-LOWERCASE-both- - - - - - together-chanting-valorously-Print-in-action-at- - - longlast-movable-type-at-breakneck-gallop- - - - - - Cummings-Boyle-Sandburg-flash-through-daredevil-commaless-Cossacks-astride-mustang-bronco- - - - vocabularies-leaning-farout-into-inky-night- - - - - picking-up-carefully-placed-phrases-with-flashing- -

Afric-teeth- -Myself-I-see-motherfather-newscope -
Optical-Writers-running-round-newhorizon-rims- -
rhythmically-Eye-Writers-writing-endless-lines- - -
for-reading-machines-more-optical-mental-more- - -
colorful-readable-than-books- - - -simple-foolproof-
Readie-Machine-conveying-breathless-type-to- - - -
eager-eyereaders-tickling-Inner-ears-dumping- - - -
Inner-ear-Eyefuls-of-wriggling-writer-right-before -
receptive-ocular-brain-portals-bringing-closer- - - -
hugging-readerwriter-now-there-is-more-mental- - -
necking-radioactivity-television-readievision- - - - -
going-on-more-moving-reading-more-moving- - - - -

The above is neither telegraphese nor a stab in
the dark at writing modernly. It is but a crude
attempt to convey the optical continuity of
reading matter as it appears spinning past the
eye out of a word-machine. It is hampered by the
connecting hyphens and columns and lacks
MOTION, the one essential of the new reading
principle.

With written matter moving before the eyes
new forms of expression will develop naturally
and surely more expressive ones, at least a technical eye-lingo of the Readie will result. The eye
refreshed will ask for more, bawl for occasional
tickling, eye-bawl, even tinted paper could be
used to help along the flow of words and thoughts;
and surely colored lighting effects on the reading
tape. One colored strand in the up-to-date binder's
stitching relieves the dull look of a book.

Useless words will go out for a long walk and
never come back into the reading language again,

they will just walk out, drop out, dim out, fade out — OUT. Writing will recover its earlier naivete, its art quality; our reading vocabulary will be hygienically circumcised and circumscis= siled. For the first time in the history of mental optics there will exist a visual Literary Language sharply separated from the Speaking Tongue. Literary language is Optical, speaking language Vocal, and the gap between them must spread till it becomes a gulf. My reading machine will serve as a wedge. Makers of words will be born; fresh, vital eye=words will wink out of dull, dis= mal, drooling type at startled smug readers here below. New methods crave new matter; conven= tional word=prejudices will be automatically over= come, from necessity reading-writing will spring full=blown into being. The Revolution of the Word will be all over but the shouting. Reading=writing will be produced not so much for its sonorific sleep=producing qualities as for its mental=eye provoking pleasures.

I have lived with five hundred years of printed books and have felt the same papyrus that Nebuc= hadnezzar might have touched, and all this time I have lived in loving wonder, a great want=to= know about words, their here and their there, their this and their that, and the most efficacious manner of administering the written word to the patient. The monks in the beginning didn't do it so badly in their illuminated manuscripts, they retained a little of the healthy hieroglyphic, all Oriental books in ideogrammatic character are delights, early colophons splendid. But what have we got in this machine age, only Bruce Rogers and more glittering comely type to make into beautifully commonplace words which can't tell us much more than the labored chisellings of the stone age, beautiful but dumb books as clumsy in their way as the Rozetti Stone.

Let's let writing out of books, give it a chance and see what it does with its liberty. Maybe beside moths there are butterflies in the core of those cloth-cased cocoons stacked away in libraries. Let them out and have a look. With reading=words freely conveyed maybe books will become as rare as horses after the advent of the auto, perhaps they will be maintained only for personal pleasure or traditional show, as the gorgeously=trapped brewery steeds of Munich. Books may go out of style as pansy parlor paintings did after the camera came along.

Let's look for literary renaissance through the Readie; a modern, moving, word spectacle. Let's have a new reading medium in time with our day, so that industrious delvers in the Word=Pile may be rapidly read and quickly understood by their own generation at least.

The Readies are no more unusual than the Talkies, and not a scratch on television. As soon as my reading machine becomes a daily necessity certainly it will be out of date. Pocket reading machines will be the vogue then, reading matter will be radioed as it is today to newsies on shipboard and words perhaps eventually will be recorded directly on the palpitating ether. But the endless imaginative possibilities of the new medium need not lead us astray. The low-brows are presently revelling in their Movies and Talkies while the almost extinct high-brow is content to sit at home sipping his thin alphabet soup out of archaic volumes of columns, mewling a little like a puling baby taking mush from the tip of an awkward wooden spoon too gross for his musical rose-buddy temperamental mouth.

Those Obfuscates who can't make out the Readies on the dim literary horizon of the day will be the first to accept them as a commonplace tomorrow and they will be the loudest in grumb- ling if anything happens to the readie mechanism to interrupt the eager optical word flow for as much as a b i l l i m e t e r - a u g e n b l i c k.

CHAPTER V

A STORY TO BE READ ON THE READING MACHINE

Harry-virtuoso-born-musical-mid-midwest-mellow-
mooing-farm-milky-mooey-farm-;-lullaby-mother-,-
chirping-jigging-Irish-father-.-Spring-red-bursting--
throated-robbins-croaking-frogs-honking-ducks-.- -
Music-singing-rails-one-Milwauke-trip-sounds- - - -
Harry-smiling-angel-faced-sound-sensitive-.- - - - -
His- -first-violin-lesson-placid-German-local-talent-
teacher-Ach-Harry-dont-jiggle-so!-Play-so!-Harry-
fiddling-idolatrous-Mooey-Ma-dishwashing- - - - -
scrubbing-floors-.-Harry-fiddling-down-all-harsh- -
uncouth-sounds-brothers-made-banging-sordid- - -

4

shiny-milk-pails- - - - - -Harry's-curls-his-individual
egg-shell-mother-bought-coffee-cup-different-from-
thick-white-uncultured-family-drinking-mugs- - - -
Mooey-Ma's-egg-shell-curly-Harry-where-art- - - -
thou?- - - -Harrys-white-gloves-first-public- - - - -
performance-church-sociable-.-Mothers-pride- - - -
mothers-throaty-teary-wetty-pride-even-after-falls-
Pearly-priced-mother-drudgery-what-price-knee- -
drudgery-knuckles-elbows-red-drudged-.-Her- - - -
Rosary-her-Harry-cross-she'd-bear-his-milky- - - -
cowlick-Harry-play-TurkeyintheStraw!-Naw- - - -
t'aint-dignified!-Harry-Give-us-Empty-Bed-Blues!-
Naw-t'aint-classical!-Ta-te-de-de-dum-ta-te-te-
ta-dumb-Harry-Empty-Head-musical-pastels-fussy-
fugues-balmy-a r i e t t a s-tinkling-tarantellas- - - -
formerly-supposed-tarantula-bite-cure-Ta-te-de-de-
dumb-Naw-no-Hot-Mama-Mammy-stuff-no- - - -
ragtime-rhythms-Ach-Harry-dont-jiggle-so!- - - - -
Neffer-vill-music-come-so!-Harry-conceitedly- - - -
masturbating-music-Harry-sprouting-sixfeetfour- -
silk-socked-Harry-.-Mother-bought-socks- - - - -
matching-Mother-made-milky-silvery-fond - - - - -
fondling-curls-Great-gift-parlor-sofa-pillow- - - - -
musician-,-lifting-eyebrows-lifting-egg-shell-little- -
fingers-Dresden-daintiness-realold-Dutch-Dresden-
China-dainty-silk-sixfoot-Harry-holding-quivering-
bow-soul-sobs-while-brothers-swilled-sows-busted-
broncos-milked-cows-.-Harry-big-boy-now-taller- -
than-three-violin-bows-yet-looking-daily-more-like-
stuffed-Department-Store-Santa-Claus- - - - - - -
demonstrating-toy-violin-.-Mother-mooing:oH,- - -
Father!-Harry-must-finish-education-Oberlin- - - -
Musical-Conservatory!-Father-chirping- - - - - - -
unmusically:-Finish-us-all-off-then!-.-Harassed- - -

Harrys-soul-sigh-lifting-eyebrows-crowfooting.- - - -
smooth-unflurried-wide-blank-forehead-into- - - -
heavenly-angelic-perplexity-wrinkles-.- - - - - - -
Misunderstood-Harry- Miserable-Ma-swapping- - -
sighful-misunderstood-miserable-glances- - - - - - -
knowing-looks-interchanged-.-Hungarian- - - - - - -
rhapsodic-adolescent-days-Harry-doing-violin- - - -
chores-while-Maw-hustled-red-sweating-panting- -
brothers-carrying-pails-around-farm.-Crucial-day- -
dawns-.-Harry-a e t a t-eighteen-Father-asks:- - - -
Whatho!-Dull-boy-work-or-play?-Harry-sighs- - - -
c a d e n z a-Maw-sobs-l a r g h e t t o-musical- - - - -
interlude-d u o-Harry-nobly-rises-occasion-plays- -
p i z z i c a t o!-Maws-savings-send-him-Milwaukee-
first-faltering-step-up-musicmaster-ladder- - - - -
restaurant-job-sawing-wooden-violin-exchange- - -
bellyfuls-beef-stew-better-than-being-pearl-diver- -
anyway-writes-Maw-only-pot-boiler-great-future- -
greater-heights-ahead-Christ-look-what-Kreisler- -
went-through-Ysaye-Micha-Ellmann-all-geniuses-. -
Harrys-curly-milky-six-socked-beauty-attracts- - -
ladies-trembling-horsd'oeuvres-acrobats-go-nuts- - -
before-cheese-course-send-him-scented-notes-bank-
notes-.-Harry-tinkles-like-street-car-conductor- - - -
through-solos-,-his-arty-eyes-above-,-loose-lipped- -
ladies-applaud-eyeing-his-thick-jiggling-brows-.- - -
browse-.-Harry-manfully-works-way-East-ladies- -
helping-heavily-.-Takes-second-selfmaking-step- - -
great-career-violin-virtuoso-almost-virtuous-meets-
night-club-proprietoress-earns-drinks-plus-food- - -
jiggles-jingles-fourteen-hour-day-including- - - - -
cocktail-teas-.-Writes-Maw-proud-progress- - - - -.
Histrionic-brunette-hairdresser-sobs-into-gin- - - -
sends-Harry-real-violets-after-Masterly-rendition--

Mendelsohns-Spring-Song-.-Harry-writes-Maw:- - -
Almost-arrived-enclose-two-pressed-violets-please-
note-tear-stains-making-big-NewYork-hit-.-Maw- -
unaided-shows-Ladies-Aid-Society-Harrys-letter- -
Tells-Father-staytohome-brothers-all-jealous-male-
relatives:-Look-our-Harry!-Pa-corrects-her:-Your- -
Harry!-.-German-professor-hears-letter-news- - - -
shakes-hoary-head:-Ach,-maybe-two-V e i l c h e n -
a b e r-Nix-Harry-jiggles-too-much-better-play- - -
Jewsharp-.-Maw-puts-Harrys-autographed- - - - -
marcelled-Metropolitan-picture-gilt-framed-atop- -
dresser-,-Paw-promptly-knocks-picture-off- - - - -
accidentally-purposeful.-Helluva-family-row- - - - -
scene-without-shifters-Maw-tear-melted-center- - -
stage-mooing-Maw-moaning-heart-picture-picture -
heart-mooey-movie-broken-huddle-over-photo- - - -
bits-.-Paw-laughs-brutishly-tells-Maw-Aw-dry-up!-
Promises-buy-new-guitly-frame-never-does-.-Maw-
submissively-stiffling-sobs-still-snuffles-.-Harry- - -
continues-playing-way-toward-gilt-framed-fame- - -
Corner-Broadway-276th.-Street-.-Broadway-finally-
triumphantly-Mawscribbled-postal--card-reads-.- -
Maw-still-unaided-shows-Ladies-Lemonade- - - - -
Society-.-Hides-postal-from-Paw-but-lifts- -   -   -
significant-highbrows-eyebrows-his-direction-just -
like-Harry's-.-Paw-too-busy-lifting-mortgage- - - -
neither-sees-nor-replies-.Harry's-getting-along- - -
short-long-six-dollars-almost-daily-nightly-.-Then- -
great-call-comes-world-sea-call-Harry-writes-Maw-
invited-join-great-sea-going-symphony-orchestra - -
under-leadership-internationally-famous-Kosher- -
Kosarin-little-wages-but-much-first-class-refined- -
sea-tea-surroundings-.-Harry-half-seas-over- - - -
groping-through-fogs-tropical-lands-hot-nights- - -

romantic-just-like-Harry-just-right-serves-Harry- -
right-.-Sends-postcard-from-beautiful-Bermuda- - -
showing-city-hall-gorgeous-rainbow-parrot-fish- - -
frieze-mentions-Bermudas-delights-reveals-his- - -
great-musical-success-two-encores-Mendelsohns- -
Spring-Song-three-encores-Pinafore-Medley-two- -
Blue-Danube-one-Merry-Widow-.-Saw-flying-fish-.-
Maw-reports-great-news-Ladies-Aid-her-cheeks- - -
flushed,like-Spring-Beauties-.-What-news-from- - -
Harry?-Surreptitious-proud-postcard-showings- - -
Great!-Just-like-Harry-remember-his-lovely-curls- -
Dear-Harry!-unforgetable-first-Church- - - - - -
performance-his-curls-posivitively-jigging- - - - -
metronomic-bow-time-.-Blessed-boy-way-off- - - -
Bermuda-fiddling-first-violin-Atlantic-liner- - - - -
renowned-international-music-master-already!- - -
Herr-Professor:-Ach-.-Bermuda-n i c h t-g u t-dot- -
dam-Englishe-beer-sour-ass-swill-Harry-jiggles- - -
chust-like-g i go l o!-.-G i g o l o-Harry-aboard-ship -
feels-superiority-over-fellow-musicians-piano- - - -
player-too-bloody-English-didn't-always-keep - -
Harrys-time-,-Traps-too-vulgar-wore-loud-ties- - -
thought-lady-passengers-stuckon-him-Harry-knew-
better-they-liked-him-best.-Fourth-member-Kosher
Kosarin's-BermudaorBust-International-Orchestra-
played-sax-pinochle-poker-etcetera-had-chronic -
catarrh-smelled-sour-picklish-.-But-hadnt-really- -
great-geniuses-crawled-up-stuckup-their-manes - -
their-lionized-heads-through-just-such-slime-?- - -
Harry-kept-aloof-like-back-home-his-nose-above- -
barnyards-still-Maw's-clinging-vine-clean-smelling-
buttermilk-boy-.-Fellow-musicians-loved-blondes- -
Harry-loved-his-Art-his-hollow-eyed-stray - - - -
straining-strained-art-impulses-After-successful - -

Bermuda-barmaid-season-Harry-could-play-M's---
Spring-Song-flawlessly-without-music-before-him--
but-continued-turning-sheets-effectively-Harry---
stood-up-tall-poplar-tree-other-three-sat-down---
insignificantly-;-Harry-shook-condescending-curls-
replying-applause-when-any-.-Lunch-time-playing-
never-his-best-felt-peckish-slightly-seasick-but----
nighttime-always-Triumph-once-knocked--'em-cold-
putting-over-Pinafore-Medley-four-encores-aboard-
specially-chartered-d e l u x e-Elks-Convention---
family-plus-trip-.-Lunch-failure-never-explained---
probably-artistic-temperament-morning-sickness--
wobbly-sea-legs-standing-too-near-terribly-food--
smelly-kitchen-galley-or-sleeping-all-night----
alongside-loud-smelling-Saxaphonist-.-Above----
such-things-Harry-towered-tremendously-scooting-
fameward.-Next-year-Buenos-Aires-run-;-hotter--
twenty-sea-days-down-trip-ten-lazy-B.A.-days---
then-twenty-back-.-Marching-madly-around-deck--
fiddling-,,Horses!-Horses!"-announcing-deck-horse-
races-miniature-wooden-horse-races-gambling-first-
class-passengers-enjoyed-quite-beneath-Harry's--
skyward-nose-;-accompanying-booming-drum---
awakening-Rio-de-Janeiro-passengers-all-first----
class-playing-,,Cheer!-Cheer!-Gang's-all-here----
whatta-hell-dowe-care?-What-ta-'ell-do-wecare--
Now!"-ceaselessly-up-down-deserted-dawn-dark--
decks-Tramp-5-A.M.-Payjama-time!-dodging----
some-shoes-shoes-from-irate-but-firstclass-----
passengers-bound-B.A.ward-.-Always-honorably--
dodging-first-class-shoes-first-class-everything---
aboard-ship-treated-almost-like-passenger-only--
once-weekly-Kosher-Kosarin's-International-Pan--
American-Pep-Band-cheered-bleak-second-class--

souls-conducting-low-kitchen-maidy-function- - - -
called-deck-dance-;-Harry-hated-such-service-but- -
gradually-forgot-horrors-thinking-what-pleasure- -
giving-himself-charitably-cheeringup-lowly-needy -
music-hungry-second-class-souls-dim-half-souls- - -
thinking-steadily-upon-other-six-week-nights-amid-
swell-first-class-passengers-pouting-cabaret- - - - -
dancers-vacationists-carrying-dollies-doodahs- - - -
tickling-away-doldrums-dreardoms-tantalizingly- -
titillating-A-One-Boy-Harry!-From-Rio-de-Janeiro-
(accent-Rye-oh)-Harry-sent-Maw-colored-card- - -
showing-Municipal-Theatre-scribbled-across-bold -
hand-writing,"South-America's-Paris-Playing-here -
now."-Truthful-Harry-James-they-were-playing- - -
South-America's-Paris-but-hardly-Municipal- - - - -
Theatre-time-Maw-made-natural-mawish-mistake -
told-Ladies-Aid-Harry-Opera-Housing-while- - - -
really-playing-back-room-sporty-Praca-Tiradentes-
restaurant-where-jovial-varnish-salesman- - - - - -
passenger-took-bunch-from-boat-celebrating- - - -
Birthday-varnishing-all-Ryeoh!-one-big-Wow- - - -
night-ashore-.-,,Playing-there-ryeoh-our-Harry- - -
his-beautiful-building"-awed Ladies-Aid-ladies- - -
intoned-,,Harry'll-adopt-Eyetalian-name-come- - - -
back-lead-Metropolitan-orchestra-little-old-New- -
York'll-get--fooled"-,-they-spoke-toothfortooth - - -
fine-Eyetalian-eye-.-,,Shouldn't-wonder!"-Maw- - - -
admitted-.-,,Ach!-Harry-Cauliflower-Head- - - - - -
playing-near-music-some-blind-pig"-said-Herr- - - -
Professor-.- -Buenos-Aires-triumph-Harry's-first- -
taste-champagne-,,They-call-me-Pan-America's- - -
Ysaye-Maw-";-boat's-name-"Pan-America"-Harry-
neglected-informing-her-.-Trip-back-Harry-played -
roulette-Miramar-Beach-Hotel-Santos-realized- - -

sinfulness-excused-grounds-great-artists-must- - - -
experience-everything-know-feel-imbibe-chance- - -
etc.-Harry-progressing-won-twelve-dollars- - - - -
intended-send-Maw-beautiful-soulful-butterfly- - -
tray-singing-like-Blue-Danube-Waltz-but-instead- -
bought-blondine-passenger-mildly-cursing-parrot- -
because-she-insisted-also-parrot's-head-same- - - -
color-hers-;-she-thanked-him-but-didnt-meet-him- -
behind-life-boat-after-midnight-supper-despite- - -
promise- -After-two-years-frothing-back-forth- - -
North-South-Atlantic-waves-waving-same-beat- - -
Maw-suggested-visit-home-.-Harry-too-busy- - - -
replied-rehearsing-Pirates-Penzance-Medley-new- -
hit-hard-hold-orchestra-up-highest-standards-all- -
weight-resting-his-broad-shoulders-new- - - - - -
pianoplayer-unusually-dumb-regretfully-must- - - -
sacrifice-personal-pleasure-considering-career- - - -
„Will-take-you-son-honeymooning-Maw-round- - -
trip-first-class-Buenos-Aires-instead-soon's- - - - -
musical-progress-warrants."-Maw-trustfully- - - -
imparted-palpitating-secret-Ladies-Aid-set-about- -
nervously-sewing-herself-bewitching-canary- - - -
colored-organdie-surreptitiously-thinking-bygone- -
days-sewing-Harry's-first-little-shirties-before- - -
bearing-greatest-living-virtuoso-bringing-him- - - -
joyously-into-canary-colored-world-all-pink-dewy-.
Harry-would-take-her-honeymooning-just-herself -
her-artist-boy-Moon-Southern-Cross-Among-all- - -
those-music-worshipping-first-class-passengers- - -
mingling-.-Maw-raised-higher-eyebrows-toward- - -
uncouth-chirping-jigging-husband-not-her-very- - -
own-creation- -Harry-hardened-into-professional- -
classical-player-ambidextrously-flicking-sweat- - -
drops-from-nose-whilst-playing-Liederstraum- - - -

soulfully-his-hot-corner-near-noisy-noisome- - - - -
annoying-kitchen-galley-never-missing-single- - - -
note-or-one-drop-sweat-.-Harry-learned-lifting- - -
arched-eyebrows-half-inch-higher-whilst-rending- -
haunting-lurking-mystic-Bohemian-Girl.-Full- - - -
passenger-lists-thrilled-Harry-triumphant-exalted -
but-measly-little-passenger-lists-thirty-wobbly- - -
tourists-dribbling-over-musty-meals-discouraged- -
artistic-endeavor-dispirited-downhearted- - - - - -
downcast-couldnt-give-his-best.-Small-cabin-list- -
small-tips- -put-whole-orchestra-outoftune- -Then- -
came-Dorothy-trippingly-fittingly-love-fashioned- -
merely-nurse-maid-chasing-two-pink-little-lucky- -
offspring-shrewd-American-merchant-located-Rio -
de-Janeiro-but-Dorothy-beautiful-dumb-blonde- - -
pacing-decks-all-day-picking-her-charges-oranges- -
Teddy-Bears-from-lee-scuppers-dragging-about- - -
endlessly-toy-autos-trains-getting-ginger-snaps- - -
deck-steward's-pantry-between-meals-Harry- - - -
thought-she-went-deck-steward's-pantry-too-often-
wanted-play-violin-her-admiration-alone-but- - - - -
orchestra-didn't-play-children's-mealtimes-she-ate-
kiddies-table-Only-time-Harry-could-concentrate- -
her-attention-nights-when-she-hung-shadowy- - - -
outskirty-among-stewards-stewardesses-other- - -
maids-watching-first-class-dance-Harry-deftly- - -
executed-many-dreamy-waltzes-Dorothy- - - - -
dedicated-bobbing-his-beautiful-virtuoso-locks- - - -
directly-her-direction-Dorothy-finally-found-out- -
his-true-feeling-True-only-two-nights-before- - - -
arrival-Rio-but-Dorothy-fast-worker-besides- - - -
ginger-snappy-deck-steward-showed-bold- - - - -
preference-other-ladies-maids-aboard-Dorothy- - -
finally-met-Harry-top-deck-beside-big-black- - - -

smoke-stacks-blacker-shadows-after-midnight- - -
supper.-Next-morning-both-showed-black-smoky- -
shadows-under-eyes.-Dorothy-met-him-both-last- -
nights-then-Harry-knew-love-put-forth-new-art- - -
spirit-put-self-soul-into-his-playing-.Also - - - -
developed-business-technique-producing-more- - -
better-tips-picked-moony-businessmen-gold- - - -
enmeshed-dowagers-big-wattles-bags-under-dead- -
bright-eyes-picking-daintily-true-born-violinist- - -
picking-his-divine-instrument-plus-plucking-purse-
strings.-Harry-became-star-picker-bowed- - - - -
profitably-Spring-Song-finales-warmly-thanked- - -
dowagers-trip-ends-pressing-five-ten-even-twenty -
dollar-bills-into-his-manly-six-foot-four-hand.- - -
These-tips-Harry-gambled-pyramided-became- - - -
known-well-known-Casino-piker-Rio-Santos- - - -
Montevideo-Buenos-Aires.-Harry-lucky-love- - - -
roulette-lottery-everything.-Dorothy-won-securely-
sheltered-Rio-nursery-waiting-one-long-month- - -
then-two-Harry-nights-twenty-days-wait-then- - - -
Harry-home-tripping-again.-Unlike-her-sailor- - -
musician-having-one-love-one-port-Dorothy-had- -
sailor-lovers-from-all-ports-but-their-Rio-visits- - -
seldom-dovetailed-so-her-dovetailing-progressed- -
without-undue-danger./.Once-after-miraculously- -
winning-eight-hundred-dollars-roulette-Harry- - -
decided-stop-ashore-six-months-Dorothy-holiday -
musical-revel-local-cabarets.-But-nervous-Dorothy-
poutingly-pointed-his-art-duty-her-new-dress- - - -
needs-hats-shoes-wherewithals-unmentionables.- - -
Together-they-spent-one-joyous-afternoon-off- - -
shopping-Harry-back-aboard-counting-twenty-six -
remaining-dollars-recalling-all-hazily-while-playing-
Auld-Lang-Syne-pushing-away-from-Rio - - - - -

remembering-too-his-firm-resolution-buying-Maw -
much-awaited-present-beautiful-Blue-Danube- - - -
Butterfly-tray-beautiful-blue-resolution-sadly- - - -
slipped-again- - - - -/When-they-laid-Maw-away-
generation-later-she-insisted-being-buried-garbed- -
old-fashioned-canary-colored-dress-she-had-never-
worn-also-directed-town-orchestra-play - - - - - -
Mendelsohn's-Spring-Song-local-violinist-leading- -
looked-like-Harry-who-couldn't-get-back-from- - -
musical-Mediterranean-tour-.Ach-said-lowly- - - -
mourner-n i c h t - g u t-jiggle-schust-like-Harry- - -
too-fast-jiggles.

(Note:The hyphenated form to suggest movement,
continuity of words, word flow, is the only one
I can think of. It is inadequate, but the imaginative
reader may get the idea of a flow of type in spite
of the awkward breaks at the line ends, unavoid-
able in linotype composition. Punctuation is
a problem which can only resolve itself
when the words are put in motion. Probably no
commas or periods will be needed and any symbol,
as, /,may be adopted for a paragraph, or spaces
of different length may satisfy the reader's eye
in place of punctuation.

The form of the Story To Be Read on A
Reading Machine suggests the abbreviated dispatches sent by foreign newspaper correspondents
to cut down cable expense, it is not offered as
a new literary style, it is merely given as an experiment in writing prose that might be rapidly
readable when passing before the intelligent, ex-
perienced eye. New forms, styles and condensa-
tions will suggest themselves. The twenty-five

words most used in English are left out entirely, sometimes to the loss and often to the gain of the text. Written in full present-day stationary reading prose this story would be 35 % longer, which would be ridiculous, it is long enough as it is; given its full quota of „Ofs" „Thes" and „Ands" Harry's little life story would occupy 35 % more space, which would be hard on the paper-growing forests and utterly unnecessary.

Statisticians have found that in a novel of 80,000 printed words the following twenty-five are used the number of times indicated:

The	5,848	As	626
Of	3,198	You	620
And	2,624	With	582
To	2,339	He	544
A	1,696	On	514
In	1,693	At	498
That	1,076	Have	494
It	973	By	480
Is	970	Not	471
I	924	This	458
For	828	Are	434
Be	677	We	423
Was	671		29,661

Aproximately 30,000 of the words used in a book, 3/8ths, or nearly one-half of its bulk, are repititions of twenty-five little words, one to four letters long, which the active modern mind skips, takes for granted, now that there is more reading and writing going on.